GENERATION
BRAVE

GENERATION BRAVE

WRITTEN BY
KATE ALEXANDER

ILLUSTRATED BY
JADE ORLANDO

THE GEN Z KIDS
WHO ARE CHANGING THE WORLD

Andrews McMeel
PUBLISHING®

Andrews McMeel Publishing
a division of Andrews McMeel Universal
1130 Walnut Street, Kansas City, Missouri 64106

www.andrewsmcmeel.com

20 21 22 23 24 POA 10 9 8 7 6 5 4 3 2 1

ISBN: 978-1-5248-6068-4

Library of Congress Control Number: 2020933413

Editor: Monica Sweeney
Art Director: Katie Jennings Campbell
Production Editor: Elizabeth A. Garcia
Production Manager: Carol Coe

CPSIA: Asia Pacific Offset Ltd.
Kowloon, Hong Kong
1st Printing
June 2020

ATTENTION: SCHOOLS AND BUSINESSES
Andrews McMeel books are available at quantity discounts with bulk purchase for
educational, business, or sales promotional use. For information, please e-mail the
Andrews McMeel Publishing Special Sales Department: specialsales@amuniversal.com.

I HAVE NOTHING BUT
EXCITEMENT FOR WHAT THE
WORLD IS GOING TO LOOK LIKE.
YOUNG PEOPLE TODAY ARE
PUTTING UP WITH LESS AND
LESS, YET AT THE SAME TIME
CREATING ROOM FOR MORE
AND MORE, WHICH I THINK IS
THE BEST COMBINATION.

—SAGE GRACE DOLAN-SANDRINO

CONTENTS

THERE'S SO MUCH ABOUT GEN Z THAT MAKES US UNSTOPPABLE AND UNAPOLOGETIC. WHAT MAKES US UNIQUE IS THE FRUSTRATION WITH PROBLEMS THAT STILL EXIST. WE'VE GOT THE ATTITUDE THAT IF OTHER PEOPLE AREN'T GOING TO TAKE CARE OF IT, THEN WE'LL JUST DO IT OURSELVES. RATHER THAN JUST TAKING A SEAT AT THE TABLE, WE WANT TO REDEFINE WHAT THAT TABLE IS.

—NADYA OKAMOTO, FOUNDER OF PERIOD

INTRODUCTION

GENERATION Z DOESN'T HAVE TIME FOR STEREOTYPES—they're too busy saving the world. Young people ages 12 to 22 are taking over social media, marching in the streets, and speaking truth to power on an international stage when they're not starting nonprofits, writing books, giving TED Talks, and inventing solutions to problems they didn't create.

The climate crisis, gun control, inequality, mental illness, LGBTQ+ rights, corruption in government—nothing is off-limits to these incredible young activists. And they're not waiting for anyone's permission or approval. The stakes are too high. The planet is dying, people are dying, and one injustice feeds another in an ever more destructive cycle.

But these activists are starting a new cycle, feeding off each other's strength and determination. The Parkland survivors' fortitude in creating March for Our Lives inspired Greta Thunberg's Climate Strike, which influenced young activists like Naomi Wadler and Jamie Margolin in the United States. Those activists are bringing to light the disproportionate effects of gun violence and climate change on minorities, which, in turn, inspires activists like Jerome Foster II and Yara Shahidi to advocate for youth voter registration.

Every person who joins the fight adds to its power with their unique experience and perspective. And together, the brave and brilliant members of Generation Z really are changing the world. But they need help. They need you. Whether you join a march or start a movement, it's time to find your voice and use it to call attention to the issues you care about. If these activists have taught us anything, it's that you can't wait for someone else to fix what needs fixing—you just have to roll up your sleeves and get to work!

ARE
ALL
SILENCE
=
VIOLENC
LOVE
RESPECT
EQUAL
E ARE
ALL
IMMIGRAN
SILENCE
=
VIOLENC
BLACK
LIVES
MATTER
VOT

CHAPTER 1

CHALLENGING THE SYSTEM

THANDIWE ABDULLAH

- ▶ Founded the Black Lives Matter Los Angeles Youth Vanguard, an advocacy group of kids age 6 to 18 that fights for justice for black youth and students

- ▶ Named one of *TIME* magazine's 25 most influential teens in the world in 2018

- ▶ Helped to create a blueprint for safe and healthy schools (known as the Black Lives Matter in Schools program), which was adopted by the National Education Association

WE CAN CHANGE THINGS, THERE'S HOPE. BUT THERE'S NOT GOING TO BE A CHANGE UNLESS WE MAKE IT. –THANDIWE ABDULLAH

One of the most amazing things about activism is that it brings together people from many different backgrounds to work toward a common goal. Maybe people are there for different reasons—a nature lover and an advocate for equality can both end up fighting for climate justice. Or maybe you're there for the same reason but took very different paths to get to where you are. But one thing is for sure: An organization is always stronger for its diversity. Change comes faster and easier when we listen to others, learn from others, and appreciate the perspective of others.

When Thandiwe Abdullah saw that a school shooter had taken 17 lives in Parkland, Florida, she was heartbroken for the students. But she wasn't surprised—she had been dealing with gun violence for years. She watched as the survivors started to speak up about gun control, an issue near and dear to her. But something was missing: voices like hers.

As a black, Muslim girl growing up in Los Angeles, Thandiwe's experience was different from that of the Parkland survivors. Parkland was a wealthy community,

A LEGACY OF STRENGTH

Thandiwe left Twitter (at least for now), but her presence is still felt by the Twitterverse thanks to her mom, who celebrates every one of her achievements on the platform. And it's no wonder she's proud of her daughter's work—activism is essentially the family business. Thandiwe's mom is Dr. Melina Abdullah (@DrMellyMel), professor of Pan-African Studies at California State University, Los Angeles. She's also one of the founding organizers of Black Lives Matter. When asked what her first protest was, Dr. Abdullah jokes that she was born on the picket line in a community where most parents—including her own—were part of the Black Power movement. Thandiwe is a third-generation female activist, but she isn't the only one. Her little sister, Amara, is also a founding member of the Youth Vanguard. She joined Thandiwe at the podium to speak at the March for Our Lives in LA and is her partner in advocacy.

Marjory Stoneman Douglas High was a good school, and the majority of the school's students were white. Gun violence wasn't really on their radar.

And that's exactly why Thandiwe joined the #NeverAgain movement—so that she could make sure the near-constant loss of black lives to guns was on *everyone's* radar. At the March for Our Lives in LA, she spoke in front of more than 40,000 people to say, "It is important that in this time, when the voices of the youth [are] being heard across the nation, that you hear from the *black* youth." Thandiwe knew that people needed to see the bigger picture.

A month later, in a speech she gave during the National School Walkout, Thandiwe reminded the crowd that guns take the lives of innocent young people all too often. She named Stephon Clark (23 years old), Aiyana Jones (7), Tamir Rice (12), Trayvon Martin (17), and Anthony Weber (16). And then she said, "It's important, when we talk about gun control, that we uplift all the black bodies that continue to be gunned down in streets and targeted in our schools." All of the young victims she named were black, and all were killed—most by police officers—while doing nothing illegal.

Thandiwe made sure that the conversation around gun violence included the fact that black people are targeted in a way that white people are not, and it begins at school. When Thandiwe was 12 years old, her school starting using police officers to perform random searches on students. The searches became more frequent after the Parkland shooting, but at no point did the searches feel random.

Even with a largely white and Asian population at the school, it was the brown, black, and Muslim students, she says, who were pulled from class most often. And it was the schools made up of brown, black, and Muslim students that had the heaviest police presence. (This, despite the fact that most school shootings have happened in predominantly white schools at the hands of white shooters.)

While searching for weapons, police confiscated highlighters, pens, and perfume and made many students feel less safe. After joining forces with LA-based student-advocacy group Students Deserve and fighting for three years, Thandiwe succeeded in ending random

REFUSE TO LIMIT YOURSELF

Do you ever feel pressure to pick just one thing and focus on it? Like you're supposed to have a one-and-only passion that pulls you in? Guess what—most people don't. Take Thandiwe, for example. She's a multi-passionate activist, fighting just as ardently for the advancement of women, the LGBTQ+ community, and Muslims as she does for black youth and students. And she finds plenty of common ground among the causes she champions. "When I march for sisterhood, I march for girls who've felt like me," she explains. "I march for all my POC sisters and folks who have felt erased. I march for those who feel too light, too dark, and unwelcome." One experience informs the other, and all of Thandiwe's work is better off for her intersectional activism.

searches in 28 schools around LA. And she's just getting started.

Eventually, Thandiwe hopes to study law and use the degree to continue her advocacy work. "I want to transform the systems that we live under from ones that oppress us to ones that empower us," she says. The relationships with other activists and organizations that Thandiwe has forged continue to strengthen her work. Her experience may be different than the experiences of people standing with her, but they'll always continue to be stronger together than they could be apart.

FOLLOW HER FIGHT:
@thandiweabdullah on Instagram and @BLMLAYOUTH on Twitter

SAGE GRACE DOLAN-SANDRINO

▶ LGBTQ+ peer educator, public speaker, artist, writer, and activist

▶ Former ambassador to the White House Initiative on Educational Excellence for African Americans during the Obama administration

ACTIVISM LOOKS DIFFERENT FOR EVERY SINGLE PERSON, AND YOU CAN BE AN ACTIVIST IN ANY WAY THAT WORKS FOR YOU. –SAGE GRACE DOLAN-SANDRINO

Sage Grace Dolan-Sandrino has been fighting the system since she came out as transgender at 13 years old. At that age, "the system" was her middle school. Although she was ready for her transition, the school wasn't. Administrators advised her to wait until summer and be herself in high school so that she wouldn't be a distraction to other students.

Unsurprisingly, that didn't work. Pictures of her transition at home spread through the school, and harassment soon followed. So, the next day, Sage came to eighth grade as her true self. "Unfortunately, I did not get the support I needed from the school," she says. "I had to use this bathroom two flights down and across the courtyard. Teachers stopped

letting me use the bathroom because I was taking so long. So I thought, 'I don't want [what's] happening to me to happen to another trans student.'" That's when she called in the cavalry.

REPRESENTATION IN FILM

One of the issues that the trans community faces is a lack of representation in movies and television. Although more trans stories are being told, trans characters are often portrayed by straight, cisgender actors. Many members of the LGBTQ+ community, including Sage, would like to see that change. She believes that art is just another conduit for activism. "I have an artistic mission to not only normalize trans identity but to normalize and bring that level of authenticity into mainstream media," she says. With a background in film at Bard College, she plans to tell trans stories as a screenwriter and producer.

Sage reached out to the Human Rights Campaign, the largest LGBTQ+ advocacy group and political lobbying organization in the country. Representatives from the organization spoke to school administrators about how to foster an environment of inclusion for LGBTQ+ students. According to Sage, not much changed at the school: "Even after the HRC spoke to them, my school rejected sensitivity and inclusion training." But things did change for Sage.

Knowing they needed to include new and varied voices in their mission to advocate for the LGBTQ+ community, the HRC reached out to her about consulting for

them. And that led to other opportunities. "I did work at the National Center for Transgender Equality and became an ambassador for the White House Initiative on Educational Excellence for African Americans," Sage says. She also worked with The National Black Coalition and The Aspen Institute, and as a GLAAD Campus Ambassador.

All of that advocacy work fueled Sage to do even more to speak up for the LGBTQ+ community, so she began writing. She's written articles and op-eds on transgender issues for *Teen Vogue* and the *Washington Post*. In one of those articles, she talks about the Trump administration's recent decisions to roll back protections for transgender people put into place by the Obama administration—protections that Sage herself had helped create.

When the Obama administration gathered several trans and nonbinary students, including Sage, to discuss discrimination in schools, they brainstormed solutions together. "Our personal experiences and lived expertise as trans and nonbinary students helped inform the May 2016 guidance on Title IX, which clarified that prohibitions on discrimination against students on the basis of their sex also included prohibitions on discrimination on the basis

TRANS PEOPLE ARE EXTRAORDINARY, STRONG, INTELLIGENT, PERSISTENT, AND RESILIENT. WE HAVE TO BE. AND WE WILL NOT STAND FOR THE PICKING AND CHOOSING OF RIGHTS. WE STILL HAVE HOPE. —SAGE GRACE DOLAN-SANDRINO

of gender, including transgender. We felt seen," she wrote.

And then the Trump administration rescinded the guidance, even as Secretary of Education Betsy DeVos looked Sage in the eye and promised that she would protect *all* students. The administration is now trying to roll back an Obama-era policy to protect transgender people against discrimination in health care by defining gender as solely a biological condition determined at birth.

The trans community was outraged by the suggestion, with many saying that they felt the Trump administration was trying to erase their very existence. They responded with the social media campaign #WontBeErased, under which tens of thousands of LGBTQ+ people have posted pictures of themselves. Sage found herself fighting the biggest system in the country—the U.S. government.

For Sage, this battle is a reminder of why she's become an activist. Organizing and speaking out doesn't just call attention to the issues, it also calls attention to necessary actions, like voting. "If young people voted in great enough numbers, we could swing every single election. We hold the power to turn the national agenda against hatred and exclusion and toward equity and inclusion." In the meantime, Sage has this advice for everyone who supports the LGBTQ+ community: "Be an ally. We must support each other and mobilize together. That is how we will win."

THE TREVOR PROJECT

More than three-quarters of trans youth experience bullying or harassment, and 41 percent of trans people consider suicide. The Trevor Project is "the leading national organization providing crisis intervention and suicide prevention services to lesbian, gay, bisexual, transgender, queer & questioning (LGBTQ) young people under twenty-five." If you or someone you know in the LGBTQ+ community is struggling or considering suicide, the Trevor Project offers immediate support. You can call the TrevorLifeline at 1-866-488-7386, text START to 678678, or chat online at www.thetrevorproject.org/get-help-now/ day or night, 365 days a year. You can also find helpful resources on the website, including the *Coming Out Handbook*.

FOLLOW HER FIGHT: #WontBeErased on Instagram

#STILLNOTEQUAL
#RETIRESEGREGATION

THE STUDENTS OF INTEGRATENYC

▸ Designing solutions for integration and advocating for their implementation in New York City public schools

▸ Creating a budding network of schools working for integration across the country through their new endeavor, IntegrateUS

MALCOLM X ONCE SAID, "EDUCATION IS THE PASSPORT TO THE FUTURE," BUT HOW CAN WE ATTAIN THIS PASSPORT IF WE ARE NOT REFLECTED IN OUR CURRICULUM?

—IMAN ABDUL, DIRECTOR OF EDUCATION AND ENGAGEMENT FOR INTEGRATENYC

School segregation ended in the 1960s, right? That's what is taught in most American schools, the very system involved in the *Brown v. Board of Education* ruling that legally ended that segregation. But if you're a student in one of America's major cities, like New York, Chicago, or Philadelphia, you know this isn't always a reality. Segregation is still costing students opportunities more than 60 years after that decision.

IntegrateNYC, a student-led movement dedicated to what it calls "real integration," is working to change that in the most segregated city in the nation. The organization's platform demands a community-designed solution to school segregation that includes the five Rs:

1. **RACE AND ENROLLMENT.** NYC public schools must provide a diverse and inclusive environment for all students.

2. **RESOURCES.** The NYC Department of Education must provide equitable distribution of resources across all of NYC's 700+ high school programs.

3. **RELATIONSHIPS ACROSS GROUP IDENTITIES.** NYC public schools must be considerate and empathetic toward the identities of all students, focus on the power of different backgrounds,

and act to build relationships between students across group identities.

4. **RESTORATIVE JUSTICE.** All NYC public high schools must be safe while free of police and military presence and metal detectors, must treat the student body as one, must protect the integrity and humanity of each student, and must help build student leaders.

5. **REPRESENTATION OF SCHOOL FACULTY.** All NYC public schools must hire faculty who are inclusive and who elevate the voices of communities of color, immigrant communities, and

WE BELIEVE IN THE POWER OF YOUNG PEOPLE TO LEAD TODAY AND SHAPE THE FUTURE.
—INTEGRATENYC

LGBTQ+ communities so that student identities and experiences are reflected in the leadership.

In an Instagram post, IntegrateNYC put it another way: "It's time for us to have fair admissions. It's time for us to get fair resources. It's time for us to see one another as powerful. It's time for us to be students, not suspects. It's time for us to learn from diverse teachers."

To achieve their goals, the members of IntegrateNYC have created social media movements, given interviews, held town halls, organized rallies, educated students and administrators on the issues, and even addressed Congress. Not only are the student members of the organization well prepared to educate the public, they're also inventive in how they do it.

On May 17, 2019, the 65th anniversary of *Brown v. Board of Education*, IntegrateNYC held

STILL NOT EQUAL

"Separate but equal" was a legal doctrine that allowed the government to get around the Equal Protection Clause of the 14th Amendment. As long as the resources offered to "both races" were equal, they were allowed to be separate. It's how legal segregation was justified. That doctrine came to an end in 1954, when the Supreme Court ruled that racial segregation in public schools was unconstitutional.

IntegrateNYC uses the hashtag #StillNotEqual to call attention to the fact that schools remain separated by race and income and that they are not now, nor have they ever been, equal. Communities of color are subject to harsher punishment, inexperienced teachers, low-quality lunches, biased curriculum, fewer sports and arts programs, a lack of advanced placement (AP) classes, and overcrowding. By fighting for real integration, the activists of IntegrateNYC are fighting for a better education for *all* students.

INTEGRATE NOW

IntegrateNYC's partner organization, Teens Take Charge (TTC), has organized weekly strikes in NYC under the banner of #IntegrateNow to protest Mayor Bill De Blasio's inaction on integration. Each strike occurs in a different location to protest the many examples of segregation in NYC public schools. Most recently, TTC rallied outside of Beacon High School, which has a largely white population who enjoy a black box theater, dance and art studios, and a film lab. Protestors demanded an end to this sort of "resource hoarding" citywide.

In what seemed like a major victory at the time, De Blasio cited the five Rs and announced his "push to diversify NYC schools" in a June 2019 article for the *New York Daily News*. He also wrote, "When I grew up, it took a judge's ruling to diversify classrooms. Now our kids steer those decisions . . . Our students remind us that real integration starts with integrating resources and creating a system that serves everyone." Unfortunately, little has been done since.

Teens Take Charge plans to hold the mayor accountable until they see real action, tweeting, "It's been 99 days since @NYCMayor's own School Diversity Advisory Group issued recommendations to integrate NYC schools, the result of 2+ years of work from experts he appointed, town halls in every [borough], and [opportunities] for community input. Instead of adopting those recs . . . He said he wants to spend THIS ENTIRE school [year] doing 'community engagement.' We are now 3 months into the school year and that community engagement hasn't started. So we'll keep showing him what community engagement looks like every Monday morning."

TOGETHER, WE ARE GROWING A NEW GENERATION OF LEADERS WHO WILL UNITE OUR SOCIETY. –INTEGRATENYC

a "retirement party" for segregation, saying "65 years is enough." In addition to rallying, members created and distributed their own newspaper throughout NYC with the lead-in, "Youth leaders demand action towards integration and equity in New York City Schools." The paper laid out their issues, their demands, and their solutions. In an Instagram post celebrating the day, IntegrateNYC said, "These are the events to look forward to, to spark change, and to enlighten the next bright mind involved in such advocacy!" By combining achievable solutions with social media momentum, IntegrateNYC has created a movement that's sure to change history.

FOLLOW THEIR FIGHT:
@IntegrateNYC on Twitter, Instagram, and Facebook

ELIAS ROSENFELD

▶ DACA recipient and immigration activist who has worked with a variety of immigration-rights groups

▶ Awarded a full scholarship at Brandeis University, where he studies political science, sociology, and law to help him advocate for immigrants

I'VE NEVER FEARED SPEAKING OUT. I KNOW THERE COULD BE CONSEQUENCES, BUT I ALSO KNOW THAT 800,000 LIVES WOULDN'T HAVE BEEN CHANGED IF PEOPLE BEFORE ME GOT SCARED. –ELIAS ROSENFELD

Imagine being woken up in the middle of the night by armed men breaking down your door to ship you off to a foreign country where you don't know anyone or speak the language. For years, that's all Elias Rosenfeld could imagine, and it kept him up at night. It wasn't a recurring nightmare—it was a very real possibility.

Elias is one of nearly 700,000 young people who are currently waiting to hear whether they'll get to stay in America, even though most have never known another home. They are the recipients of DACA, or the Deferred Action for Childhood Arrival program, which shields young immigrants from being deported by providing them with renewable, two-year permits.

Those who received DACA status had to meet a number of qualifications, including being brought to the United States as children. Most recipients were brought over when they were so young that they can't remember their birth country. Some fled violence, which would be waiting for them if they were sent back. But with DACA, they were safe.

President Barack Obama signed the program into law in 2012, which is the same year that Elias learned that he had become undocumented. His mother held the L1 work visa that brought Elias and his sister to America from Venezuela when he was 6 years old. And when kidney cancer

LIES FROM THE WHITE HOUSE

It's hard for people to champion immigration programs like DACA when the president of the United States himself is spreading disinformation. In addition to other untrue statements, President Trump once tweeted, "Many of the people in DACA, no longer very young, are far from 'angels.' Some are very tough, hardened criminals."

The truth is, the rigorous screening process for DACA means that Dreamers are actually more likely to be upstanding citizens than many natural-born Americans. Criminal records are immediately disqualifying, so for Dreamers, breaking the rules could mean deportation. Applicants also had to be actively working, pursuing an education, or honorably discharged from the military—in other words, contributing to American society.

took her life, her visa was automatically voided. Elias had no idea until he tried to apply for his learner's permit several years later.

By then, he was already politically active. He interned at a state senator's office before high school and advocated for changes to health care laws for immigrant children. While the Dream Act (the legislation from which DACA recipients got their nickname: "Dreamers") was being considered, Elias launched the organization United Student Immigrants to advocate for undocumented students. But the 2016 elections solidified his commitment to activism. That was the year presidential candidate Donald Trump promised to end DACA. In response, Elias volunteered for Hillary Clinton's campaign.

In 2017, President Trump fulfilled his promise to end DACA as part of his broader nationalist agenda. The lives of those 700,000 people were suddenly thrown into chaos. By this time, many recipients were older and had careers and families, car payments and mortgages. They, like Elias, now had to fear ICE (Immigration and Customs Enforcement) breaking down their doors, and so did their spouses and employers.

That fear is what made Elias want to take even stronger action. While many DACA recipients tried to stay under the radar, he made sure that people heard stories like his. "If people don't know our stories, then they don't see the complexity of the issue and they won't pressure their legislators," he says. He's given interviews and spoken at rallies, but he's also gotten involved in advocacy groups like @FWD_us and @MIRACoalition and interned for progressive Senator Elizabeth Warren.

On top of that, Elias studies political science, sociology, and law at Brandeis University under a full scholarship—something that couldn't have happened without DACA. "It's exhausting. It can feel like I'm always under pressure," Elias says. "But then I think about the people who fought to get DACA passed in the first place. Going to college was impossible for them. DACA made it possible for me. That's what drives me. I don't want people to have to walk in my shoes."

Elias chose Brandeis because of its commitment to social justice, saying, "I knew the school would have my community's back, for sure." And they did. Before Trump announced the end of DACA, Brandeis president Ron Liebowitz sent a letter urging him not to. The letter

WE NEED EVERYONE

One of the anti-immigration arguments is that immigrants will take the jobs of hardworking American citizens. That's just not true. In fact, most business owners agree that immigrants are an integral part of a healthy economy. Not only do many of our greatest innovators come here from other countries, but many Dreamers own businesses themselves that employ other Americans.

Plus, as American citizens have fewer children, we actually have more jobs than people to fill them. That's especially true for caretaking professions. We have many more elderly people than young people to care for them. Blocking immigration—especially for those who are already contributing members of American society—is self-sabotage that usually has more to do with prejudice and racism than with actual concern for American jobs.

said, "Here at Brandeis University, we value our DACA students, who enrich our campus in many ways and are integral to our community. Reversing DACA inflicts harsh punishment on the innocent. As a nation founded by immigrants, we can, should, and must do better." The government may not have done better, but Elias is trying to. His fate, and the fate of 700,000 others, now rests in the hands of the Supreme Court and activists like Elias who hope to sway its opinion.

FOLLOW HIS FIGHT: @AdvocatElias on Twitter

YARA SHAHIDI

▶ Founded Yara's Club, a digital meetup for high school students to discuss social justice issues, self-improvement, and education

▶ Created Eighteen x 18 to motivate young voters to participate in all elections

▶ Worked with the Obama White House on STEM initiatives and the First Lady's Let Girls Learn education initiative

WHEN WE LOOK AT WHAT WE'RE AIMING TO ACHIEVE, I FEEL LIKE IT'S IMPORTANT TO UNDEFINE IT ALL AND TO MAKE IT SO EXPANSIVE THAT YOU CAN'T HELP BUT TO FIGHT AND ADVOCATE FOR EVERYONE. –YARA SHAHIDI

Who says that you have to pick one thing to care about? Not Yara Shahidi! And she's tired of everyone pigeonholing Generation Z into two camps: the social-media obsessed and the one-issue warriors. In choosing to make a difference wherever and whenever she can and using social media as a tool to inspire and educate, Yara is "undefining" youth activism. "We all get to contribute to this larger movement of equity, in whatever way we find natural to us," she says. And when you tap into those natural inclinations, you tap into your real power to create change.

Scroll through Yara's Instagram page and you'll find posts of her gleefully eating breadsticks next to posts calling out U.S. Customs and Border Protection for human rights violations. And as far as Yara's concerned, that's how it should be. "There's power in just displaying joy," she says, and it doesn't mean that you're not socially engaged. Although some accuse her generation of hashtag activism (essentially, being "all talk"), Yara knows the true impact social media can have.

"Social media matters. Twitter matters, Instagram matters," she explains. "I now no longer have to be concerned with just the stories my newspaper is giving me, or CNN. I'm learning about iconic activists not through my school system but through Twitter, through following this other person that I admire or am inspired by. It means that there's this new exchange of information happening." She says that "awareness is the first step," and young activists are using their social media influence to bring much-needed attention to their causes.

Yara's many causes include representation, immigration, education, LGBTQ+ rights, body positivity, gun control, and climate change. But she's especially focused on helping young people understand the importance of voting, which can affect all of these issues. Not only did she turn her eighteenth birthday party into a voting party, complete with registration booth, she also founded an organization dedicated to making politics accessible to her generation.

Eighteen x 18 (@eighteenx18 on Twitter and Instagram) hopes to break the barrier between young people and politics so that they're more likely to get out and vote. On its social media pages, you'll find posts and stories about young activists, current events, and common political terms and processes so that everyone can feel comfortable talking about issues and heading to the polls. But the most important thing Yara wants you to remember about voting is, "There's no such thing as an off year." Your vote makes a difference to the issues you care about in every election, big and small. (If you need a visual reminder, just pick up the Yara Barbie!)

ACTRESS, ACTIVIST, COLLEGE STUDENT, BARBIE DOLL

By the time Yara was asked to skip first grade, her mother knew she was a force to be reckoned with. Today, she's the lead in her own TV series (Freeform's *Grown-ish*), the founder of a political platform, an activist fighting for equity on all fronts, and a student at Harvard University. Oprah Winfrey has said that she expects Yara to run for president one day. She'd certainly have all the inside info, having worked with former First Lady Michelle Obama on education initiatives. (Mrs. Obama even wrote Yara a college recommendation letter.) Yara has a lot of honors under her belt, but one in particular stands out: her very own role model Barbie doll, complete with her signature "VOTE" tee shirt!

JUST LIKE MOM

If you believe what you see in movies, there's a lot of eye rolling and door slamming between teenage girls and their moms. But anyone who's been watching Yara knows how close she is to her mom, Keri, who is usually right next to her on the red carpet or in magazine interviews. Yara says that she and her mom are "basically the same human in different bodies," and that her mom is "genuinely always right."

KERI SHAHIDI

Keri is the one who taught Yara that giving back is an important part of life. When Yara was little, her mom told her, "You have three jars: You have saving, you have spending, and you have donating. What do you want to put in each jar?" So, from her first paycheck, Yara understood that when you get some, you give some. And she's been applying that advice to her activism, using her privilege and platform to highlight inspiring people and important causes.

That's also thanks to Keri, who made sure Yara knows that her opinion is worthy. "As a young girl, there are so many pressures, especially as a woman of color. She taught me to understand that I am qualified for any of the conversations that I'm a part of, whether it's with executives or a school principal. I'm supposed to be there." It's on that foundation that Yara has built her multifaceted activist efforts—she knows that she can tackle any issue she wants to and make a difference. And so can you!

When you look around at all of the amazing young activists in the world, it's easy to think you're not doing enough. But you are! Yara wishes people would realize that and celebrate themselves more often. "So many times we look at other people and we are able to acknowledge all of the amazing things that they're doing," she says, "but hardly do we do that for ourselves."

Try this: Without comparing yourself to anyone else, take a step back and think about all of the little ways you've tried to make a difference in someone's life. And remember, you don't have to lead a rally to make a difference. You can hold the door open for a stranger, compliment a friend's shoes, invite the new kid to sit with you at lunch, or even take your dog for a long walk. If your goal is to make someone happy, you're making a difference. Celebrate that!

FOLLOW HER FIGHT: @YaraShahidi on Twitter and Instagram

JOSHUA WONG

▶ Nominated for the Nobel Peace Prize in 2017, at the age of 21

▶ Played a leading role in getting U.S. politicians to pass the Hong Kong Human Rights and Democracy Act

PERHAPS SUCCESS IS FAR OFF. BUT EVEN IF WE COULD TURN BACK THE CLOCK, I WOULD STILL CHOOSE CIVIL DISOBEDIENCE. IT IS A RESPONSIBILITY OUR GENERATION BEARS, AND WE WILL NOT HOLD BACK UNTIL THE DAY DEMOCRACY ARRIVES. –JOSHUA WONG

Growing up in America, it's easy to take your rights for granted. If you disagree with your government, you can say so in a news article, stage a peaceful protest, vote for candidates who share your beliefs, or even run for public office yourself. No matter what, you get a say. And by using your voice, you can make a huge difference.

That's all Joshua Wong wants for Hong Kong—the right to have a say. Right now, Hong Kong's leader, or chief executive, is chosen from a pool of candidates who are pre-approved by the Chinese government in Beijing. But communist China is very different from the more democratic Hong

ONE COUNTRY, TWO SYSTEMS

Although Hong Kong (officially called the Hong Kong Special Administrative Region of the People's Republic of China) is part of China, it was a British colony for more than 150 years. It was returned to China in 1997, but it still has its own currency, legal systems, and civil liberties. That's because its return came with a loophole—a constitutional principle called "one country, two systems"—so that no one would get whiplash from switching political systems overnight. But Hong Kong's time under British rule had other effects that Beijing isn't crazy about, namely differences in education, culture, and lifestyle. Put simply, Hong Kongers have a lot more freedom than the mainland Chinese have. And Beijing would like to change that.

FEAR FOR THE FUTURE

When the United Kingdom handed back Hong Kong, the region was assured special rights and freedoms through the "one country, two systems" principle. But that agreement expires in 2047, and no one really knows what happens next. That's why Joshua feels it's so important to take action now—he wants to ensure that Hong Kong's future is a free one. If Beijing is allowed to continue tightening its grip on Hong Kong over the next several years, then there's a good chance that 2047 will see a communist Hong Kong. Joshua knows the stakes, and he's not giving up. He writes, "I continue to believe that Hong Kong, as the freest part on Chinese soil with the strongest faith in democracy, can still make a difference."

HONG KONG MAY BE SMALL, BUT ITS PEOPLE MAKE IT GREAT.

–JOSHUA WONG

Kong region, which means that their chief executives aren't usually people Hong Kongers would choose, given the chance. And Joshua thinks it's about time that changed.

Ever since high school, Joshua has noticed that the pro-Beijing picks for leader of Hong Kong are quietly trying to chip away at the freedoms Hong Kong was promised. And he's not having it. When the government tried to require that schools teach subject matter praising the Communist Party of China, Joshua saw it as a move to brainwash Hong Kong's youth. Together with classmate Ivan Lam Long-yin, Joshua started Scholarism, a pro-democracy student activist group focused on educational, political, and youth policy. In just one year, he went from handing out leaflets to leading a political rally of more than 100,000 people.

The government dropped the proposed curriculum, and Joshua had discovered what a little civil disobedience could do. So, in 2014, Scholarism joined forces with the Umbrella Movement—a series of protests that brought Hong Kong to a standstill to demand the right for the region to pick its own leaders. (The rebellion got its name from the umbrellas protesters used to protect themselves from the police's pepper spray.) "The peaceful, 79-day demonstrations failed to win any major concessions from Beijing," writes Joshua, "but they did show us the potential our generation had to make a meaningful difference."

That's when Joshua decided to try fighting the government from the inside. Together with members of Scholarism, he founded a new political party. That party, called Demosistō, calls for Hong Kong to become permanently democratic when

JOSHUA WONG

the clock runs out in 2047. His goal was for members of Demosistō to run for and win local office and to gain the majority in the legislature. But Beijing is putting up roadblocks wherever it can.

The Chinese government has begun to demand loyalty from all candidates, and they believe that the members of Demosistō want an independent Hong Kong. Joshua and the others have repeatedly made clear that they don't want full independence—just universal suffrage (aka, the vote). But one by one, pro-democracy candidates have been barred from running, including Joshua himself.

If Beijing had hoped to stop pro-democracy sentiment by quashing the candidates, they were sorely disappointed: 2019 saw the strongest pro-democracy protests yet. As Joshua said, "Adversity will only sharpen our wits and make us more strong-willed, resulting in the political awakening of more Hong Kongers, not to mention the international community's support." The world saw Beijing's move for what it was—an attempt to control Hong Kong. And *no one* is having it.

More international allies are stepping up to help, thanks in large part to Joshua's new role as unofficial ambassador for a democratic Hong Kong. He's been traveling all over the world to shore up support. Thanks to his testimony in front of Congress, the United States passed the Hong Kong Human Rights and Democracy Act (which requires the United States government to impose sanctions on Chinese and Hong Kong officials for human rights abuses). So the next time you're tempted to think that your voice doesn't matter, think of the impact that Joshua has had, even as Beijing tries to keep him quiet.

SECRET AGENT MAN

In an effort to discredit Joshua, pro-Beijing newspapers spread rumors that the United States had groomed him to be a "political superstar" and that he was working with the CIA. Some even called him out as a threat to communist rule, which made him a target of both police and individual attackers. He was often arrested and held when other protesters were let go, even spending months at a time in jail. But all it did was strengthen his resolve.

FOLLOW HIS FIGHT: @joshuawongcf on Twitter

CHAPTER 2

CREATING A SAFER WORLD

THE NEWTOWN ACTIVISTS

▶ Living with the long-term effects of experiencing one of the deadliest school shootings in U.S. history

▶ Inspired by the Parkland activists to lend their voices to the fight for gun control

> ## PARKLAND WAS A REMINDER THAT WHAT HAPPENED IN NEWTOWN IS STILL HAPPENING, AND NOT NEARLY ENOUGH HAS CHANGED IN THE ALMOST SIX YEARS BETWEEN THE TWO TRAGIC EVENTS. –NATALIE BARDEN

On December 14th, 2012, a gunman opened fire on Sandy Hook Elementary School, killing twenty first-graders and six educators in one of the deadliest mass shootings in American history. The town has yet to recover. In the years since, it has mourned the losses, demolished the school, and asked for privacy and routine on each anniversary in an attempt to move on. But many residents—including some of the 400 other students who were in school that day—have no desire to move on. Not until the policies that enabled the shooting change.

Realizing that activism was the only way forward for them, high schoolers Jackson Mittleman (@jmittleman25) and Tommy Murray (@tmmurray1000) became co-leaders of the Junior Newtown Action Alliance to work toward gun violence

ECHOES OF TRAUMA

Since the Columbine shooting in Colorado, active-shooter drills have become common practice at American schools. Companies are creating bulletproof backpacks and whiteboards. Metal detectors are posted at entrances, and security guards watch school hallways. Teachers go to work mentally and emotionally prepared to stand between danger and their students. These are the echoes of the national trauma mass shootings inflict.

Today's kids are forced to grow up in this traumatic environment by adults who cling to antiquated gun laws. Jason Mittleman sums up this divide in one tweet: "Gun owners often say that imposing safe storage laws is a burden on their right to own a firearm. I say that it's a burden on kids' right to live to practice active shooter drills and go to school every single day fearing they might not come home." Unless we put an end to the gunshots, we'll never stop hearing the echoes.

@humansofnewtownct. With personal stories, the Instagram account illustrates that one gun does not hurt only those who are injured or killed but rather an entire community. The organization and its members also have an active Twitter presence, highlighting events, legislation, opinions, and both survivors and victims of gun violence.

Natalie soon realized that, as the sister of one of the victims, she could do more to bring national attention to the issue. Watching the Parkland survivors, she thought, "if these kids are able to speak about this topic so soon after this tragedy, I can join them by adding my voice." She began accepting interview requests, attending summits on gun violence, and even writing op-eds for national publications like *Teen Vogue*.

Natalie finds comfort in the other activists and the power of their shared purpose. Survivors of school shootings are forever connected by their trauma, fear, and grief, but today, they're also connected by their drive to make sure no one else has to go through what they went through. "Each time I do an interview, I feel physically drained from the emotional toll," she writes, "but standing together, among my peers, I see how strong we are." Although she meant it figuratively, 350 residents of Newtown,

prevention. (Tommy's mom, Po, co-founded the adult-run branch of the club, the Newtown Action Alliance.) Natalie Barden (@NatalieBarden), whose brother Daniel was killed in the shooting and whose parents are also activists, joined the boys for their first few meetings.

But when the Parkland shooting happened, the club filled with new members. They quickly prioritized creating a social media presence, starting with

Connecticut, also stood with the Parkland survivors at March for Our Lives in Washington, D.C.

In addition to joining strikes and rallies, the JNAA has organized voter registration drives and began advocating for candidates who support safer gun laws. They created a platform of demands that includes: banning semiautomatic magazines that can hold dozens of bullets, closing loopholes in background-check laws, raising the minimum age for purchasing a gun to 21, and providing a route for courts and law enforcement to temporarily remove guns from people who pose a threat to themselves or others.

Although Connecticut passed sweeping gun-control legislation after the Sandy Hook shooting, the federal government didn't budge. The JNAA plans to change

that. "Up until recently, our generation hasn't been able to voice our opinions," said Garrett Marino, a student at Newtown High who attended Sandy Hook. "So if there was ever a time for something to change, it's going to be now." Natalie knows it will happen. "The movement of gun-violence prevention is not going to die out," she writes, "because there are thousands of kids who have been forced to take action after suffering terrible losses . . . We stand together, and we are not backing down until we feel safe in our own country."

REMEMBERING THE VICTIMS

Charlotte Bacon, 6 years old
Daniel Barden, 7 years old
Rachel D'Avino, 29 years old
Olivia Engel, 6 years old
Josephine Gay, 7 years old
Dawn Hochsprung, 47 years old
Dylan Hockley, 6 years old
Madeleine Hsu, 6 years old
Catherine Hubbard, 6 years old

Chase Kowalski, 7 years old
Jesse Lewis, 6 years old
Ana Márquez-Greene, 6 years old
James Mattioli, 6 years old
Grace McDonnell, 7 years old
Anne Marie Murphy, 52 years old
Emilie Parker, 6 years old
Jack Pinto, 6 years old
Noah Pozner, 6 years old

Caroline Previdi, 6 years old
Jessica Rekos, 6 years old
Avielle Richman, 6 years old
Lauren Rousseau, 30 years old
Mary Sherlach, 56 years old
Victoria Leigh Soto, 27 years old
Benjamin Wheeler, 6 years old
Allison Wyatt, 6 years old

FOLLOW THEIR FIGHT:
@humansofnewtownct on Instagram and @Junior_NAA on Twitter

AUTUMN PELTIER

▶ Appointed chief water commissioner (protector of the water) for the Anishinabek Nation, a political advocacy group for 40 First Nations across Ontario

▶ Named one of BBC's 100 most inspiring women in the world and nominated three times for the International Children's Peace Prize for her work protecting clean water

ONE DAY I WILL BE AN ANCESTOR, AND I WANT MY DESCENDANTS TO KNOW I USED MY VOICE SO THEY CAN HAVE A FUTURE. –AUTUMN PELTIER

Think about how often you use water. Not only do you drink it but you also bathe in it and brush your teeth with it. You wash dishes with it, wash your dog with it, swim in it, and make your mac and cheese with it. Spend just one day counting all the ways you come into contact with water and you'll be astonished by the number.

Now imagine that your water is toxic and you can't use it at all. How much harder did your day just get? And what if you had to live without clean, running water for years? That's what the First Nations communities of Canada have been dealing with, and that's why indigenous clean-water warrior Autumn Peltier is speaking out.

The first time that Autumn understood the importance of clean water was the first time she didn't have access to it.

BOIL-WATER ADVISORIES

When a government issues a boil-water advisory, it's telling you that your community's water is contaminated and could make you sick. You can (and should) sanitize the water by boiling it, but these advisories usually recommend that you stick to bottled water and disposable plates whenever possible (which makes taking a shower tricky). When Autumn began advocating for clean water, 100 First Nations communities were under boil-water advisories, some for decades. Thanks to advocates like her, that number has fallen by half.

WIIKWEMKOONG FIRST NATION

She was just 8 years old and attending a ceremony on a First Nations reserve about an hour and a half away from home. She was startled by signs in the bathroom that said, "Don't drink or touch the water" and "Boil water." Her mom explained that the water was toxic, as it was on so many reserves.

It was in that moment that Autumn understood what her great aunt, famous water warrior Josephine Mandamin, had been fighting for. Not only was Josephine chief water commissioner for the Anishinabek Nation before Autumn, but she also founded the Mother Earth Walk (an annual walk around the Great Lakes to raise awareness for clean water) and helped establish the Great Lakes Guardians Council.

Autumn considered her great aunt, who died in February of 2019, her inspiration and biggest mentor in protecting the water. She helped Autumn find her voice, which she's used at conferences all over the world. In addition to

JOSEPHINE MANDAMIN

speaking at the Children's Climate Conference in Sweden, Autumn has addressed world leaders at the United Nations more than once. In these speeches, she makes her cause clear, saying, "Canada is not a third-world country. But here, in my country, the indigenous people live in third-world conditions." And when she had the opportunity to confront the leader of her country about it, she did.

In 2016, Autumn was chosen to give Prime Minister Justin Trudeau the gift of a ceremonial copper water bowl at the First Nations' annual winter meeting. She gave him a piece of her mind instead, saying, "I am very unhappy with the choices you've made." She made it clear that she was referring to his support for oil pipelines. As she often says, "We can't eat money or drink oil." Trudeau promised a tearful Autumn he would protect the water, and he seems to be making some progress. At last count, the Canadian government had resolved more than half of the boil-water advisories.

Today, Autumn draws strength from her great aunt's legacy and her final words of advice. "Before [Josephine] passed away, she told me, 'Don't let anyone stop you. And don't care what people say—just keep on doing the work,'" Autumn remembers. "So that's exactly what I'm going to do."

NOW IS THE TIME TO WARRIOR UP AND EMPOWER EACH OTHER TO TAKE A STAND FOR OUR PLANET.
−AUTUMN PELTIER

LIVING WATER

Part of Autumn's passion for protecting the water comes from her ancestors. Autumn is Anishinaabe-kwe from the Wiikwemkoong Unceded Territory on Manitoulin Island in Ontario, Canada. In her culture, they believe that water is a living being. As she told the UN, "For years and years, our ancestors have passed on traditional oral knowledge that our water is alive and our water has a spirit." This is a common belief among indigenous peoples worldwide. A Maori tribe in New Zealand recently fought for and won legal human rights protections for their river—something Autumn would like to see become a trend. In fact, she hopes to go to law school and fight for exactly that.

KIDS ALL OVER THE WORLD HAVE TO PAY FOR MISTAKES WE DIDN'T EVEN MAKE. THIS IS OUR FUTURE, WE'RE THE NEXT ELDERS, WE'RE THE NEXT LEADERS. −AUTUMN PELTIER

FOLLOW HER FIGHT:
@autumn.peltier on Instagram and @Waterwarrior1 on Facebook

THE PARKLAND SURVIVORS

▶ Survived a school shooting and turned their grief and fear into a movement called #NeverAgain, with the goal of changing ineffective gun laws

▶ Organized the March for Our Lives, for which 1.2 million people in more than 800 cities turned out in support

IF THEY CONTINUE TO IGNORE US, TO ONLY PRETEND TO LISTEN, THEN WE WILL TAKE ACTION WHERE IT COUNTS. WE WILL TAKE ACTION EVERY DAY IN EVERY WAY UNTIL THEY SIMPLY CANNOT IGNORE US ANYMORE. –DELANEY TARR

On February 14, 2018—Valentine's Day—a 19-year-old man used an assault rifle (a military-grade gun) to terrorize his former school, Marjory Stoneman Douglas High School. The shooting lasted only 6 minutes and 20 seconds but left 17 people dead and 17 more wounded. The emotional wounds are immeasurable. Many surviving students still suffer from survivor's guilt and post-traumatic stress disorder (PTSD). They'll spend the rest of their lives trying to heal unseen scars, which isn't made easier by knowing that the world is watching.

After the shooting, friends and family gathered to mourn their loss at a candlelight vigil. High school junior

Cameron Kasky (@cameron_kasky) looked around at the tearstained faces, and he got angry. Angry that someone had taken his friends. Angry that high schoolers had to face this kind of tragedy. Angry that lawmakers weren't doing anything

ENOUGH IS ENOUGH

While the Parkland shooting was a tragedy, it wasn't unexpected or unavoidable. There have been more than 230 school shootings in the United States, and that number goes up every year. They're common enough that students all over the country practice active-shooter drills. But many politicians refuse to consider gun-control laws. Coincidentally, these same politicians often take money from the NRA (the National Rifle Association, a gun-advocacy group). The Parkland activists say #EnoughIsEnough. Their Peace Plan calls for C.H.A.N.G.E.:

Change the standards of gun ownership

Halve the rate of gun deaths in 10 years

Accountability for the gun lobby and industry

Name a director of gun violence prevention

Generate community-based solutions

Empower the next generation

With protests, rallies, interviews, and even tweets, they are demanding that lawmakers stop taking money from the NRA and commit instead to taking these steps against gun violence.

it's not the time yet to talk about gun control. So here's the time that we're going to talk about gun control: March 24." When the day came, the Parkland survivors "talked" to 200,000 people who had gathered to protest gun violence in Washington, D.C.— not to mention thousands more watching at home on TV and social media. Altogether, 1.2 million people in more than 800 cities turned out to support the movement.

By then, fellow students Jaclyn Corin (@JaclynCorin), Matt Deitsch (@MattxRed), Ryan Deitsch (@Ryan_Deitsch), Brendan Duff (@Brendinid), Aalayah Eastmond (@AalayahEastmond), Emma González (@Emma4Change), David Hogg (@davidhogg111), Lauren Hogg (@lauren_hoggs), and Delaney Tarr (@delaneytarr) had joined the fight. After they delivered their speeches at the rally, these courageous kids took the fight nationwide with a tour they called Road to Change.

about it. He decided right then and there to take action, inviting classmates Alex Wind (@al3xw1nd), Alfonso Calderón (@Alfonso_Cal), and Sarah Chadwick (@Sarahchadwickk) over to brainstorm. That night, they created a movement Cameron called #NeverAgain. Within days, they had a goal, a plan of action, and thousands of followers.

On February 18, 2018, Cameron announced the March for Our Lives by saying, "One of the things we've been hearing is that

David wants young people to do more than march. Too many politicians stand in the way of gun reform, and the only solution is to vote them out. "We can have all the walkouts we want," he says, "but if we don't walk to that ballot box and make our voices heard, these politicians aren't going to listen." Emma adds, "Get out and vote. If

THE POWER OF SOCIAL MEDIA

Social media has made all the difference in the #NeverAgain movement. From that first night, when the survivors set up their Twitter profiles, they've used a mixture of channels to organize events, post updates, and even confront members of Congress. Thanks to their social media savvy, they've been able to reach millions of people with their message and create huge turnout for things like the Enough! National School Walkout and the March for Our Lives.

Sarah Chadwick thinks social media is the perfect platform for activism: "We learn from other teenagers, and that's how our generation has become so politically active, inspiring, and educated. We're learning from each other." Both Sarah and Delaney consider it "one of the safest ways to find community." The Parkland survivors know that, despite some of the negatives, social media can be a powerful tool for good. It all depends on how you use it.

you can't vote, then register other people to vote. Get people to the polls; make sure that people who need to vote can vote." And that's exactly what she's been doing.

In the summer of 2018, she and other Parkland survivors visited 80 communities in 24 different states and registered more than 10,000 new voters. In the end, they and like-minded voters flipped the House of Representatives, giving Democrats (who tend to champion gun reform) the majority. With that win under their belt, they're focused on the November 2020 elections. They won't stop until gun violence is a

thing of the past. As Delaney put it, "We are no longer just high school students, that much is true. We are now the future, we are a movement, we are the change."

Everything the Parkland survivors have accomplished—all of the rallies and reforms—began with them getting together in Cameron Kasky's living room and spit-balling ideas over snacks. They knew that, together, they would be a force stronger than any one of them could be alone. In their grief, the Parkland survivors turned to each other and decided to change the world.

REMEMBERING THE VICTIMS

Alyssa Alhadeff, 14 years old
Scott Beigel, 35 years old
Martin Duque, 14 years old
Nicholas Dworet, 17 years old
Aaron Feis, 37 years old
Jaime Guttenberg, 14 years old

Chris Hixon, 49 years old
Luke Hoyer, 15 years old
Cara Loughran, 14 years old
Gina Montalto, 14 years old
Joaquin Oliver, 17 years old
Alaina Petty, 14 years old

Meadow Pollack, 18 years old
Helena Ramsay, 17 years old
Alex Schachter, 14 years old
Carmen Schentrup, 16 years old
Peter Wang, 15 years old

FOLLOW THEIR FIGHT: @AMarch4OurLives on Twitter, @marchforourlives on Instagram, and www.marchforourlives.com

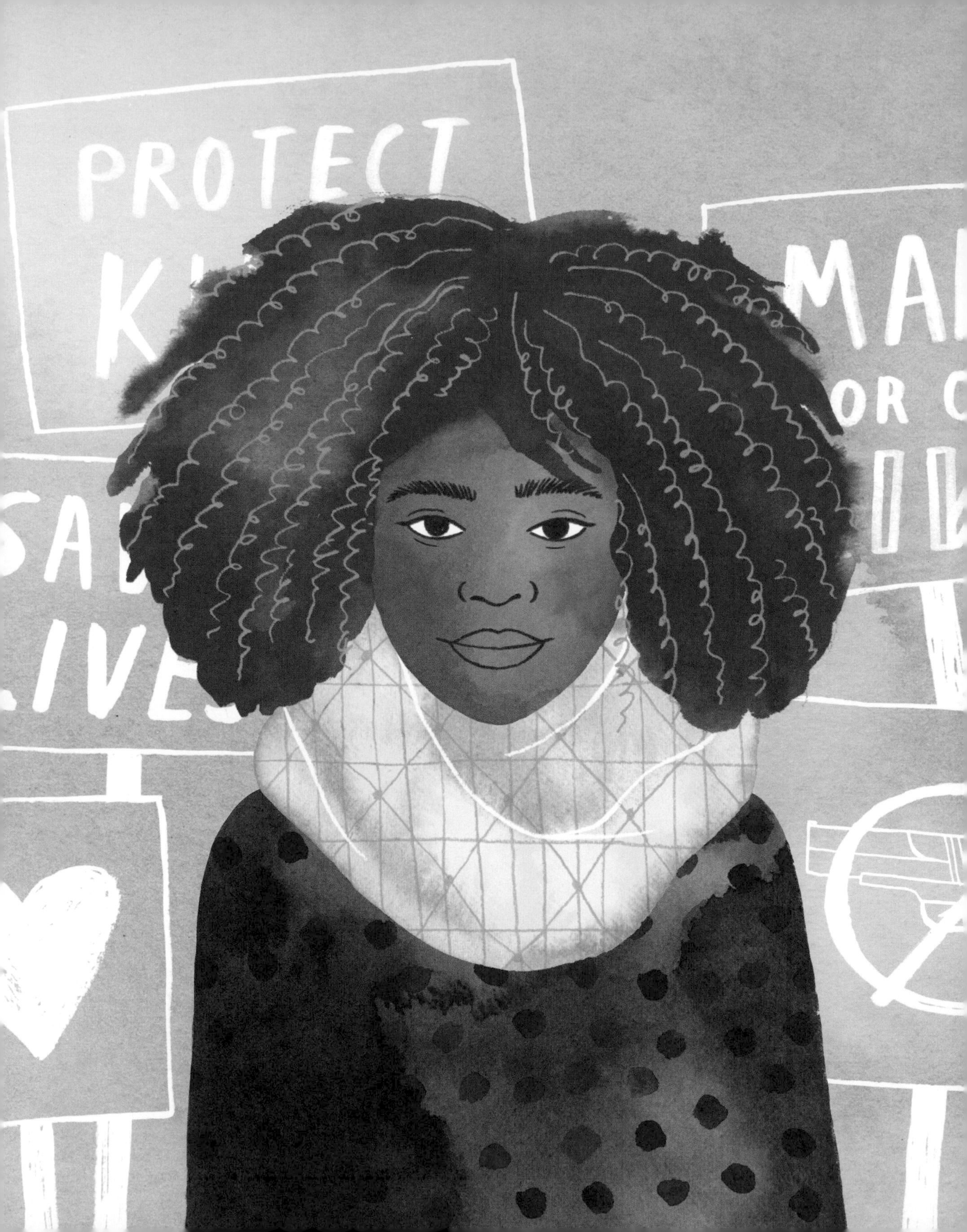
PROTECT

NAOMI WADLER

▶ Spoke for underrepresented African American girls lost to gun violence at the March for Our Lives in Washington, D.C., at the age of 11

▶ Using her powerful voice to tackle social justice issues that affect girls of color

> **MY FRIENDS AND I MIGHT STILL BE 11, AND WE MIGHT STILL BE IN ELEMENTARY SCHOOL, BUT WE KNOW. WE KNOW LIFE ISN'T EQUAL FOR EVERYONE, AND WE KNOW WHAT IS RIGHT AND WRONG. WE ALSO KNOW THAT WE STAND IN THE SHADOW OF THE CAPITOL, AND WE KNOW THAT WE HAVE SEVEN SHORT YEARS UNTIL WE, TOO, HAVE THE RIGHT TO VOTE.** –NAOMI WADLER

Have you ever felt like someone was underestimating you? Naomi Wadler knows the feeling. She was being honored by *Teen Vogue* as one of their "21 Under 21" when she said, "Every time I go and speak and every time I do something, I feel underestimated or I see that I am being underestimated." And this was *after* she gave a speech in front of millions of people at the March for Our Lives in Washington, D.C., spoke at the Women in the World summit at Lincoln Center, and interviewed with Ellen DeGeneres on national TV.

The fact that she was only 11 years old and standing 4 feet, 6 inches tall probably didn't help. "How could she know, at such a young age, what the world needed?" her detractors thought. "How could she understand enough to even form an opinion?" Many adults forget how much they understood by middle school. And many more overlook what kind of world they've created for younger generations.

In the last few years, thousands of young activists have risen up to do what these underestimating adults will not, and Naomi is one of them.

When Naomi discovered that her mom's friend had lost his daughter in the Parkland shooting, she knew that she had to take action. Through tears, she told her mom, "I want to do something. What do I do?" But then she figured it out herself. In the days that followed, Naomi decided to organize a student walkout at her elementary school in Virginia with her friend Carter Anderson. Unlike all the other walkouts, hers was eighteen minutes long—seventeen for those who lost their lives in Parkland, and one for Courtlin Arrington, the African American girl murdered in her Birmingham, Alabama, classroom whom no one was talking about.

That extra minute caught the media's attention, and news organization NowThis came knocking on Naomi's door for an interview. Next thing she knew, George Clooney was calling to invite her to speak at the March for Our Lives! She didn't know what to say, until her mother reminded her of all the questions she'd been asking over the years— questions about why the media treat white victims and black victims so differently. During her speech, Naomi reminded the crowd of those African American women and girls lost to gun violence who don't make the front page. "For far too long, these names, these black girls and women, have been just numbers," she said. "I am here to say 'never again' for those girls, too."

Since that day, Naomi has become even more dedicated to lifting up the voices of girls of color. In addition to interviews

UNEXPECTED ALLIES

When Naomi took the stage at March for Our Lives to talk about gun violence affecting girls of color, a lot of people assumed that she came from a black, liberal, D.C. family. But Naomi's parents are both moderate Republicans living in the suburbs. Plus, her mom is white, and her dad is a card-carrying member of the NRA. And neither is her biological parent—Naomi's mom adopted her from Ethiopia. In other words, Naomi is not what anyone assumed she was (which should tell you something about making assumptions). But the need for gun control is something that the whole family agrees on.

and speeches, she's using her new social media accounts to share their stories. (Because Naomi's a preteen, her parents get the final say about when and how she can use social media.) You can also find her on ellentube, interviewing inspiring people about how to find your voice and make a difference for her new web series, *DiversiTEA with Naomi Wadler*.

Having people underestimate her certainly hasn't stopped Naomi from changing the world. And it doesn't have to stop you, either. Trust your voice (even when it shakes). You know more than you think you do, and you can change as much as you think you can.

MANAGING AN ACTIVIST

Naomi's mom, Julie, didn't mean to become the manager of a rising activist. "Nobody was prepared for this," she says. "She wasn't prepared for it. I wasn't prepared for it. No one in our lives was prepared for it." The fame and speaking engagements and interviews all came so fast that Julie didn't have time to think about what was happening. But she adapted quickly, hiring a lawyer to draft contracts, buying web addresses, and filing paperwork to create the Naomi Magic foundation (naomimagic.com).

She also chauffeurs Naomi to speeches in her minivan, makes sure homework's getting done and bedtimes are observed, and, of course, puts all of those speaking fees straight into a college savings account. Although she's now a manager, she's also just a proud mom, amazed by the incredible advocate her daughter has become. Talking about Naomi's speech, she says, "You could see that what she said mattered—and that is an amazing thing to watch."

REMEMBER, YOU DON'T HAVE TO TRAVEL AROUND THE COUNTRY SPEAKING ON A NATIONAL PLATFORM. REAL CHANGE STARTS LOCALLY; REAL CHANGE STARTS WITH YOU. –NAOMI WADLER

FOLLOW HER FIGHT: @NaomiWadler on Twitter and Instagram

CHAPTER 3

STOPPING CLOCK on CLIMATE CHANGE

FIONN FERREIRA

▶ Winner of the 2019 Google Science Fair for developing a method to remove microplastics from water

▶ Working on scaling his method for use in wastewater plants and on ships so they can filter microplastics as they sail

IT'S NOT ONLY ABOUT MY METHOD. I WANT TO GET OTHER PEOPLE INSPIRED TO LOOK AT CREATIVE THINKING AND CREATIVE WAYS TO SOLVE PROBLEMS. BECAUSE, OF COURSE, THIS IS ONLY ONE PROBLEM. THERE ARE MANY MORE LEFT TO SOLVE. –FIONN FERREIRA

Have you ever noticed that the more you focus on a problem, the harder it is to solve it? They say the best thing to do when you're stumped is to stop thinking for a bit. Take a shower, have a nap, or—better yet—go for a walk. Walking in nature is a powerful problem-solving remedy, shown to boost not only your mood but also your brain function. Just ask Fionn Ferreira—the inspiration for his microplastics removal project struck while he was kayaking around the Irish coast.

Growing up on a remote island in southern Ireland, Fionn spent a lot of time exploring the beaches and waterways.

So, when he learned about microplastics polluting the water, he immediately set out to find a solution. "This problem is personal," he says, "because I saw the effects of microplastic pollution on our environment all the time in Ireland."

The first step in finding any solution is to understand the scope of the problem. A natural-born scientist, Fionn analyzed the plastics he found along the shore, mapping their numbers,

MICROPLASTICS 101

Microplastics are, as you would imagine, really tiny plastic particles. And thanks to our overuse of plastics for the last few decades, we now eat, drink, and breathe these particles pretty regularly. Although no one knows yet how bad that is for us (scientists are working on it), we know that it's not good.

Part of the reason these particles are everywhere is because of how much plastic makes its way into the ocean. Once there, it breaks down and gets mistaken for food by sea creatures. And those sea creatures are part of our food chain, which means those microplastics make their way back to us. Although Fionn's discovery is a huge step toward combatting microplastics, he says that his project isn't the solution. "The solution is that we stop using plastic altogether."

He thought, "This is interesting. Maybe if I added vegetable oil to an expanse of water with plastics in it, well, maybe plastics would stick to this vegetable oil." He was right, but he quickly realized that filling the oceans with vegetable oil wasn't a great solution. Fionn was not deterred—he knew he was on to something. He just needed that last piece of the puzzle. And he found it, not when he was looking for it but while working on something else entirely (a high school science experiment).

That missing piece was a magnet. By mixing the vegetable oil with magnetic powder (which creates a ferrofluid), Fionn is able to pull out both the oil and the particles using a simple magnet. In the process, inky black, plastic- and oil-filled water suddenly becomes clean and clear.

types, and locations. Then, he researched existing solutions—only to discover that there weren't any. That's when Fionn decided to create the solution himself.

Fionn had been puzzling over the problem for a while when he stumbled upon an intriguing sight—a rock covered with oil-spill residue and microplastics. This rock was not only a symbol of the greater problem of pollution but also a clue about how to deal with microplastics. Why were the oil and microplastics both sticking to the rock? After a bit of research, Fionn discovered the answer: Both plastic particles and oil are nonpolar, and in chemistry, like attracts like.

When talking about it, Fionn smiles and says, "I think it should be included in those 'satisfying things to watch' videos that you often see advertised on YouTube."

Fionn tested his method on the ten most common types of plastic, from milk bottles to washing machine fibers and microbeads (which have been banned in the United States since 2015). And after thousands of tests, he discovered that his method consistently removed 87 percent of microplastics from the water. Now, with a little outside help, he's ready to put his method to good use in wastewater plants and on ships.

Thanks to his win at the Google Science Fair, he's had no shortage of people who want to work with him. He even received a congratulatory tweet from the president of Ireland that read, "May I convey my congratulations to Fionn Ferreira on winning the @googlescifair, with his project examining options for removing micro-plastics from the oceans. His problem-solving, environmental awareness and independent thinking are an inspiration to us all." And that's exactly what Fionn hopes to be—an inspiration to others to get creative when faced with a problem. The more minds at work, the more problems we solve!

TESTING HIS LIMITS

In a YouTube video for the Plastic Soup Foundation (an environmental nonprofit), Fionn describes his scientific methodology like a seasoned chemistry professor. But he also stops to laugh at his parents' reactions to his sometimes explosive experiments. Having no access to a lab to test his method, he set out to build his own lab equipment in his bedroom, including a spectrometer and a microscope. "I made lots of prototypes, believe me," he says, "some of which exploded, some caught fire. And my parents weren't very pleased with me doing this in my room."

He also took apart the washing machine to find fibers to use in his analysis. "It never worked correctly afterwards," he chuckles. "It always left dirty smears on our washing. So, my parents, again, were not very happy with me." Without his parents' everlasting patience, Fionn may never have discovered his successful method. Thankfully for them, though, Fionn is out of the house now and has actual labs in which to experiment at the college he attends, University Groningen in the Netherlands.

FOLLOW HIS FIGHT:
@fionn.ferreira on Instagram and @FionnFerreira on Twitter

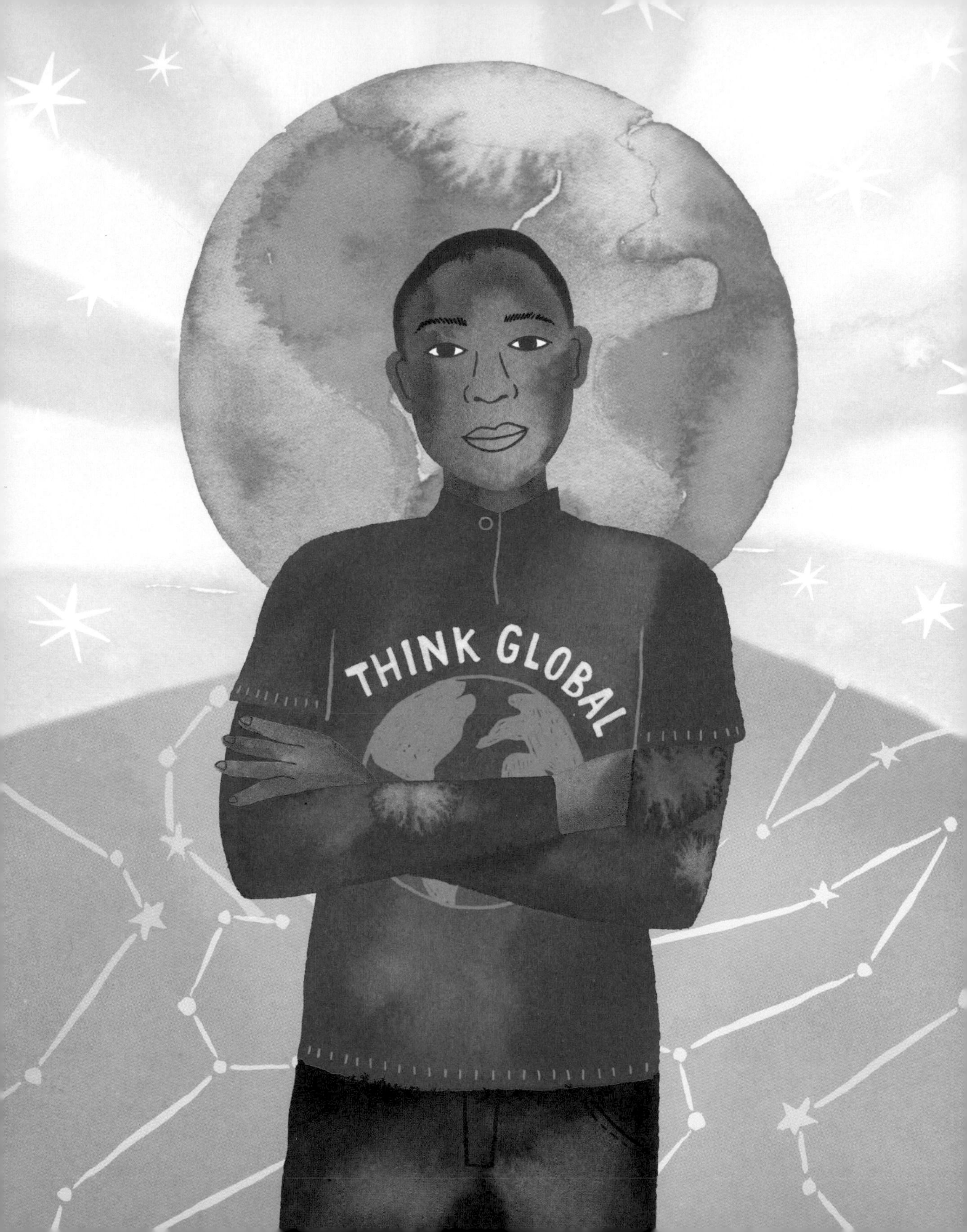
THINK GLOBAL

JEROME FOSTER II

▶ Organizes and strikes with Fridays for Future to demand legal action on climate change

▶ Founded OneMillionOfUs, an organization dedicated to getting out the youth vote

WE SHOULD NOT BE SEARCHING FOR HOPE, WE SHOULD BE SEARCHING FOR ACTION AND DEMANDING URGENT ACTION FROM OUR ELECTED REPRESENTATIVES NOW. –JEROME FOSTER II

They say that one of the ways to discover your passion is to list everything you enjoy and look for common threads. Jerome Foster II would have absolutely no problem doing that. Though clearly multitalented, Jerome has found a way for all of his projects to revolve around one thing: combatting climate change.

Jerome's résumé is almost intimidating at first glance. He's an organizer for Fridays for Future, an advocate for Zero Hour, a National Geographic Explorer, a Smithsonian Ambassador, founder and editor-in-chief of the *Climate Reporter* (his global news blog), founder and executive director of OneMillionofUs (a voter-registration campaign), and founder and CEO of TAU VR (a virtual reality company). He's also an AP high school student.

While his packed schedule certainly seems like a product of passion, Jerome would argue that it's not—it's a product of fear. "I am NOT passionate about the climate crisis," he says on Twitter. "I am scared of the climate crisis. It is in the same way that I am not passionate about gun violence but rather I am scared of being gunned down in my own classroom."

Jerome believes that every one of us needs not only to change our behavior but also to advocate for sweeping legislative change. Smaller plays, like recycling at home, won't make the kind of impact we need to make in the time we have left to make it, he says. He also believes that his generation is going to be the one to get the job done.

THE CLIMATE-CRISIS EXPERIENCE

As a resident of Washington, D.C., Jerome has an even harder job of convincing people to care about climate change. Not only do partisan politics play a big role in denying the science of climate change—and D.C. doesn't have voting representation in Congress anyway, a whole separate issue—but the district doesn't experience much in the way of extreme weather thanks to its temperate location. And what residents in a temperate climate don't experience for themselves, they may have a hard time believing exists at all.

That's one of the reasons that Jerome created his virtual reality company. With a bit of genius coding on his part, his virtual reality software allows users to experience the consequences of climate change, up close and personal. They can move through oceans filled with plastic, visit an oil refinery, or watch glaciers melt in Iceland. He knows the scenarios might not change the minds of real climate-change deniers, but he hopes that others will gain a better understanding of the problems our planet faces.

After joining Zero Hour, Jerome decided to spend his Friday mornings striking for climate change outside the White House. He spent his Friday afternoons at the Capitol Building, interning with Representative John Lewis, a Democrat from Georgia. Jerome was worried about splitting his time between the two most powerful buildings in D.C., saying, "I thought they wouldn't support it because I'm literally striking against the U.S. government." But it turns out that he had nothing to be nervous about. When the House Select Committee on the Climate Crisis noticed Jerome striking outside the White House, they actually asked him to speak at an event.

Being that close to the action, Jerome couldn't help but notice how voter turnout affected the legislation that gets passed. But currently only one in five young people turn out to vote. Jerome founded OneMillionOfUs to change that.

In chapters all over the country, organizers with OneMillionOfUs educate,

energize, and—most importantly—register young people to vote. And they have their sights set on the 18.36 million potential voters turning 18 before the 2020 presidential election. To help encourage these new voters, organizers talk about issues where their vote can effect the most change, including immigration reform, gender equality, racial equality, gun violence, and climate change. As Jerome says, "Change starts in the streets and ends at the polls."

While his organizers work on increasing voter turnout across the country, Jerome is still raising awareness in D.C. Recently, he's joined forces with award-winning actress Jane Fonda for a new initiative, called Fire Drill Fridays (@FireDrillFriday on Twitter, Instagram, and Facebook). The name comes from Greta Thunberg's now-famous call to action: "We have to act like our house is on fire, because it is." Jane adds, "This is a collective crisis that demands massive collective action." And she'll be advocating for that action at the Capitol every Friday alongside indigenous leaders, experts, community members, and climate activists like Jerome.

SCORE ONE FOR THE MOVIES

Schools may be lacking lessons on climate change, but Hollywood sure isn't. In fact, Jerome credits James Cameron's movie *Avatar* with alerting him to ozone depletion. Not only are many actors and celebrities vocal advocates for climate-change causes, they're also educating the public through entertainment. In addition to high-budget sci-fi hits like *Avatar*, you've got explosive action movies like *The Day After Tomorrow* and even heartwarming family films like *WALL-E* and *Tomorrowland* offering warnings about the climate crisis.

Learning about the consequences of climate change while munching on popcorn is better than nothing, but it may not have quite the same impact as studying them in school. Jerome's working on that, too. One of his goals in striking is to advocate for the Climate Change Education Act, which would require that climate change be incorporated into schools' science curriculum in all grades.

RATHER THAN DEBATING WHETHER THIS CRISIS IS REAL, WE NEED TO BE FINDING SOLUTIONS TO SOLVE IT. —JEROME FOSTER II

FOLLOW HIS FIGHT:
@jeromefosterii and @OneMillionOfUs on Twitter and Instagram

HELENA GUALINGA

▶ Advocates for the freedom and protection of indigenous peoples and their lands

▶ Marched and spoke during the NYC climate strike on September 20, 2019

TOGETHER WE HAVE TO STAND UNITED BECAUSE WE ARE ALL LIVING ON THE SAME PLANET. AND NOW WE HAVE TO SAVE HER. –HELENA GUALINGA

If you've ever learned about Greek mythology (or read the Percy Jackson books), you know what the Hydra is—a terrifying, many-headed sea monster. Just think of climate change as the Hydra. Its heads include environmental issues like endangered species and melting ice caps, but they also include social justice issues like racism and income inequality. You may see separate sets of razor-sharp teeth snapping at you, but they all belong to the same monster.

Now picture all of the climate activists battling together, swords in hand. Isra Hirsi leads the attack on the head that leaves people of color vulnerable. Jamie Margolin fends off the one that's counting down to zero. Jaden Smith swipes at the head that spews pollution and poison. And Greta Thunberg throws everything she has straight at the body of the beast.

Helena Gualinga is part of that fight, swinging her sword against the head that steals healthy, sacred land from indigenous peoples only to destroy it for profit or political gain. Helena is a member of the Kichwa nation and Sarayaku community, one of 370 million indigenous peoples that live all over

GROWING UP GUALINGA

Growing up in the Ecuadorian Amazon certainly had its perks. Helena didn't have a jungle gym to play on—she had an actual *jungle* to play in. Whether the night sky offered a warm rain or a blanket of stars, she was happy on her people's ancestral lands. And that connection with the land is exactly what she's trying to protect. Scroll though her Instagram account and you'll find beautiful pictures of her home, hopes for its healthy future, and updates on her fight.

THE LUNGS OF THE WORLD

It's no coincidence that the Amazon rainforest is called "the lungs of the world"—its 2.124 million square miles is capable of absorbing about 25 percent of the world's carbon dioxide emissions and releasing life-giving oxygen in its place. But thousands of square miles have burned in 2019 alone, and the fires still rage.

These fires weren't lit by accident. Farmers and ranchers purposely set fire to the rainforest to clear land for their crops and livestock. With the blessing of Brazil's authoritarian president Jair Bolsonaro, they're burning the lungs of the world for profit. And they're threatening and even killing anyone who stands in their way. Until these people are held accountable for the rainforest's destruction, indigenous peoples and the lands they care for will never be safe.

the world. Like other people of color, indigenous peoples are disproportionately affected by climate change.

Helena calls indigenous peoples "the protectors and the guardians" of the Amazon. The beautiful lands that they have spent centuries—if not millennia—caring for are being invaded and destroyed for oil, logging, ranching, and mining. And worse, the protectors are being oppressed and killed. Just recently, indigenous forest guardian and activist Paul Paulino Guajajara was murdered by illegal loggers in the Brazilian Amazon.

One of the biggest problems Helena sees is that so few people are aware of what indigenous peoples are facing—it doesn't make international news. But it should. "In my territory, we protect the global climate from destruction, and that's why indigenous peoples' rights to their territory go hand in hand with climate justice," she says. "That is why I feel I have to do this, for my people and for the world."

When asked how people in other countries can help, she answers, "It's important to be aware of what is happening and why."

And that has become Helena's mission. She wants to get everyone talking about what's happening in the Amazon. Right now, the bad guys are using the darkness to their advantage. She shines her light on Ecuador so that those who are destroying her homeland have nowhere to hide.

Now, Helena isn't Joan of Arc. She's not literally battling the bad guys with sword in hand. The sword Helena wields in the fight against climate change is her voice. In speeches and on social media, she documents the fight for the Amazon. She calls out the corporate greed, the political corruption, the destruction, and the violence. And she calls for the protection of indigenous rights. "By protecting indigenous peoples' rights," she writes, "we protect billions of acres of land from exploitation."

WE ARE THE VOICE OF THE FOREST.
—HELENA GUALINGA

THE ORIGINAL CARETAKERS

Indigenous peoples are the original owners and caretakers of their particular region—they are the people who came before settlers or colonizers. Many of these groups have a deep respect for nature and a unique understanding of how to care for it. For generations, they have coexisted with it in sustainable and symbiotic ways, their traditions carefully preserved and passed down. But there's one centuries-long tradition that Helena would like to end: the fight to protect that heritage. In an Instagram post on November 6, 2019, Helena wrote, ". . . if big companies and our governments don't stop stealing our lands, if they don't stop killing our leaders. Our elders' fight and my generation's fight will be passed on to them. They will be the next targets. We can't let that happen."

FOLLOW HER FIGHT:
@SumakHelena on Twitter and @helenagualinga on Instagram

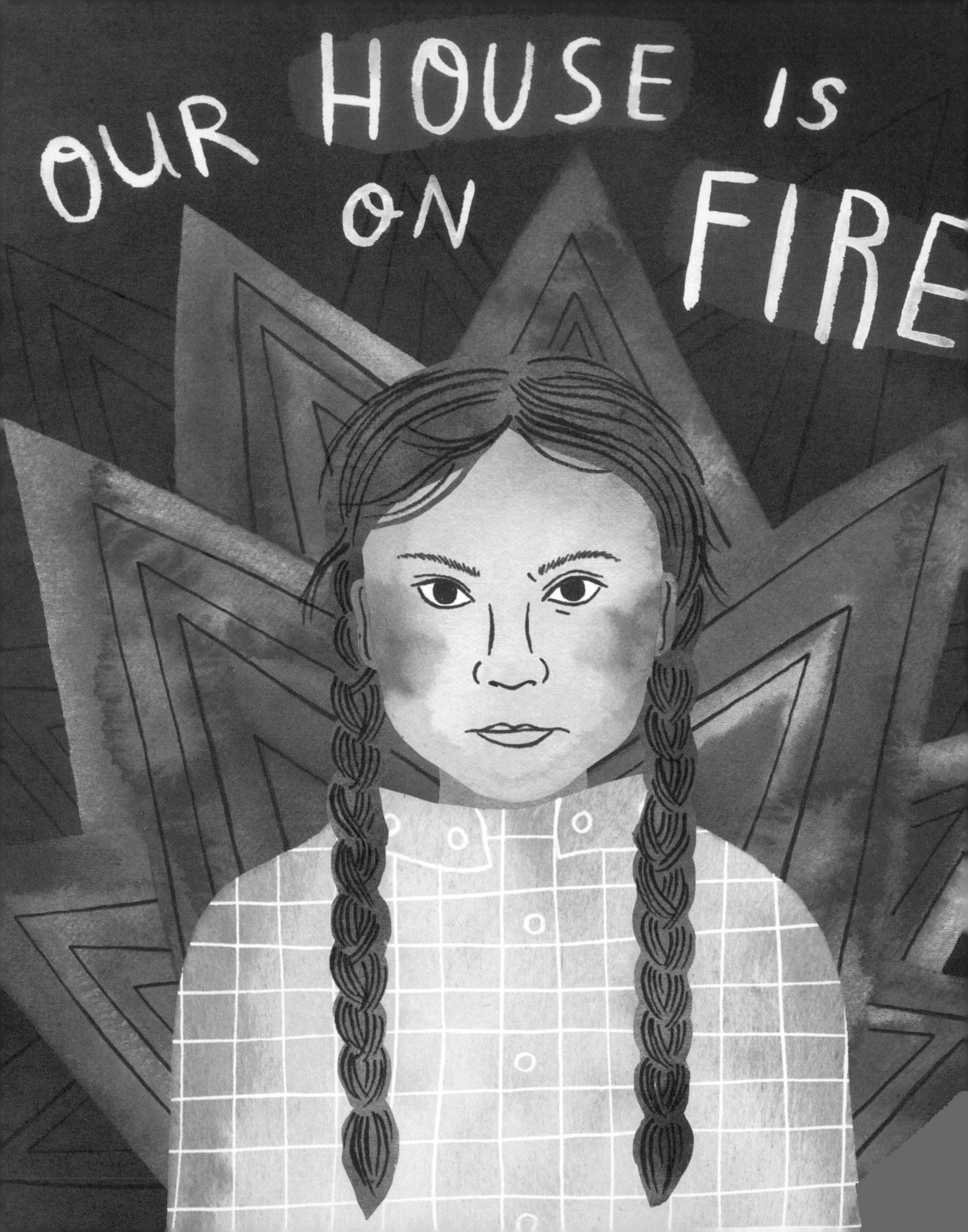
OUR HOUSE IS ON FIRE

GRETA THUNBERG

▶ At 16 years old, she led nearly 8 million people across 185 countries in the largest climate strike in history

▶ Nominated for a Nobel Peace Prize and named *TIME* magazine's 2019 Person of the Year

WE SHOWED THAT WE ARE UNITED AND THAT WE YOUNG PEOPLE ARE UNSTOPPABLE. —GRETA THUNBERG

Do you think you're too young to make a difference? Or too small? Or too shy? So did a 15-year-old girl named Greta. But, by finding a cause she believed in, she found her voice. And now she's using it to energize millions of people, challenge powerful world leaders, and save the planet, one peaceful protest at a time.

When Swedish-born activist Greta Thunberg (pronounced TOON-bairk) first learned about climate change at the age of 8, she was wracked with worry. Human activity has led to pollution, depletion of natural resources, animal habitat destruction, and emitted millions of tons of carbon into the atmosphere, causing the earth to warm at a dangerous rate. With animals dying, oceans swelling, and deadly storms raging,

WALKING THE WALK

Greta tries to reduce and even reverse her impact (or "carbon footprint") on the planet in any way she can. But traveling to international conferences and rallies can make that tricky. When she was invited to speak in Switzerland, she chose to spend 32 hours on a train rather than hop on a short flight. Crossing the ocean, however, would take a little more creativity. To attend the United Nations Climate Action Summit in New York, she spent two weeks sailing across the Atlantic on a schooner that ran on wind, solar power, and underwater turbines. Her total environmental impact: zero.

Greta understood that human beings were destroying their own future, and they didn't seem to care. For years, Greta lived with a sense of dread, so depressed that she could barely eat or speak.

Finally, she confided her fears in her parents. They were in awe of their daughter's passion and confidence—and her ability to win an argument. It didn't take long for Greta to convince her world-traveling mom to give up airplanes and her dad to give up meat to help reduce the family's carbon footprint. She herself became vegan (someone who doesn't eat or use any animal products like meat, milk, or leather). By making a difference at home, she realized she could make a difference anywhere.

The only question was how to make that difference. She found inspiration in the survivors of the Marjory Stoneman Douglas High School shooting in Parkland, Florida, who organized a walkout to protest the lack of gun control. With her parents' permission, Greta decided to stage a similar protest for three weeks leading up to the Swedish general election. The goal: to convince people and politicians to take real action. She needed them to see that climate change was "a matter of life and death."

On August 20, 2018, Greta skipped school to sit outside the Swedish parliament with flyers and a simple, hand-painted sign that read "Skolstrejk för Klimatet" (School Strike for Climate). She wasn't alone for long, though. By day two, she had plenty of people standing with her on the pavement *and* on social media. Their support gave her the confidence she needed to do even more.

Less than a month after her first day outside parliament, Greta bravely stood in front of hundreds of people (and all of social media) to give her first-ever speech at the People's Climate March rally in Sweden. Her three weeks were up, but nothing had changed. So she announced that she would continue to protest every Friday. Her speech ended with a call to join her: "Everyone is welcome.

GRETA'S SUPERPOWER

Greta lives with Asperger's syndrome, a diagnosis on the autism spectrum that makes it harder for her to socialize and communicate. But communicate she does! Repeatedly, in front of hundreds of thousands of people at a time, and to awe-inspiring results. Some people have tried to use her diagnosis to tear her down, even calling her "mentally ill." Greta didn't flinch. Instead, she took to Twitter to address the "haters," writing, "I have Asperger's syndrome and that means I'm sometimes a bit different from the norm. And—given the right circumstances—being different is a superpower." Greta credits her Asperger's for the tireless passion, clarity, and focus that makes her protests possible.

Everyone is needed." And join her they did, in a worldwide movement they called #FridaysforFuture.

Greta continued making impassioned speeches, inspiring change, and calling out the grownups who weren't doing enough. At the United Nations Climate Change Conference in December 2018, she said, "Since our leaders are behaving like children, we will have to take the responsibility they should have taken long ago." A month later, at the World Economic Forum, she said, "I don't want you to be hopeful. I want you to panic. I want you to feel the fear I feel every day. I want you to act. I want you to act as you would in a crisis. I want you to act as if the house is on fire, because it is." Her fearless calls for change earned her a reputation for speaking truth to power and a nomination for the Nobel Peace Prize.

Greta was right to think she could make a difference. On September 20, 2019—

just a year after her first protest—Greta led 4 million people across 161 countries in the largest climate strike in world history. A week later, it was 7.6 million in 185 countries. And the numbers just keep growing.

Greta is still young, small, and shy. But she knows that just on the other side of her fear is the power to move mountains, and so she pushes through it. She says, "I don't want to be heard all the time, but if there is anything I can do to improve the situation, then I think it's a very small price to pay." Just imagine what you could do if fear weren't a factor!

BATTLING ONLINE BULLIES

When you publicly fight for something important, you're bound to have more than your fair share of bullies. And social media has made it all too easy for bullies to hurt people from the comfort of their own home. Greta is no exception. Greta chooses to focus on the people who have her back—and there are plenty of those! Supporters include Canadian Prime Minister Justin Trudeau, German Chancellor Angela Merkel, and the Pope. She knows that there will always be people who don't believe in what you're doing. But real change comes from believing in yourself.

FOLLOW HER FIGHT: @GretaThunberg on Twitter and Instagram

JAMIE MARGOLIN AND THE ZERO HOUR ACTIVISTS

▶ Founded Zero Hour, an organization dedicated to demanding climate justice to help save humanity from itself

▶ Honored by a number of organizations (including *Seventeen* magazine, the *Today Show*, and the BBC) as a girl who is changing the world

IT'S SO IMPORTANT FOR THE YOUNGER GENERATIONS—ESPECIALLY GENERATION Z—TO SPEAK OUT ON CLIMATE CHANGE, EVEN IF SOME ADULTS UNDERESTIMATE YOU. –JAMIE MARGOLIN

Jamie Margolin has always had strong opinions about climate change. But as a young, mixed-race girl, she was getting used to adults ignoring her concerns. She never let the patronizing "don't worry" smiles get to her, though. She knew that the real problem was that these adults weren't just ignoring *her*. They were ignoring climate change entirely—even as Earth's fate ticked closer and closer to the point of no return.

Jamie decided it was time to take matters into her own hands. "We must speak out because it is our lives that are on the line," she writes. "It is our future and there is nothing more powerful than youth saying that we will not lay down and accept this fate that is being laid out for us by the powerful among our parents' generations." She immediately got to work.

FINDING PEOPLE LIKE YOU

Finding like-minded people can be tricky for young activists. If you're still searching for where you fit in, remember that the whole world is at your fingertips. Literally. Nadia found Jamie on Instagram after reading her essay (entitled, "An Open Letter to Climate Change Deniers") in *Teen Ink* magazine. In fact, many of the members of Zero Hour didn't meet in person until they were ready to plan their march on Washington. When you see people who inspire you online, think about how you can emulate their efforts at home. You never know what you can accomplish together!

Although she didn't have much luck rallying people in her local community, Jamie didn't let it deter her. Instead, she realized she needed to think even bigger. At age 15, she decided to organize a march on Washington that the adults couldn't ignore.

Friends Madelaine Tew, Nadia Nazar (@nadiabaltimore), and Zanagee Artis (@ZanageeArtis) joined Jamie (@Jamie_Margolin) in creating Zero Hour, an organization dedicated to climate justice. The name comes from the urgency of the cause: "There are zero hours left to take action," says Jamie. Today, more than a dozen strong, capable teens fill out the Zero Hour team. Their website (thisiszerohour.org) boldly declares, "We know that we are the leaders we have been waiting for!"

The Zero Hour activists stand for "intersectional climate justice," meaning that they believe that climate change is directly related to equality and justice for disadvantaged groups. Sea levels are rising and threatening to drown cities, ice is melting and releasing long-slumbering viruses, and dangerous natural disasters are becoming the norm. And the people who are most likely to suffer from these climate-change consequences are women, people of color, low-income communities, indigenous peoples, and people with disabilities.

Just think of it in terms of evacuation. Evacuating before a natural disaster can mean the difference between life and death. But it requires physical ability to pack up and leave, transportation, and savings to pay for hotels, food, and clothing (because you won't be able to work and earn money). We know that natural disasters are getting worse and more frequent because of climate change. And we know that not everyone will be able to get out of harm's way. That's why we have to be concerned with *both* climate change *and* the people it's most likely to affect.

The Zero Hour activists aren't just fighting to save the planet. They're fighting to prevent the kinds of disasters that take lives and devastate communities.

To make a difference on one issue, they have to tackle them all—climate, economic inequality, racism, sexism, and colonialism. And that takes more than just protests. As Jamie says, "We can't pretend like we have the luxury of choosing one solution." Education and outreach are a big part of the Zero Hour playbook.

The team created a campaign called "Get to the Roots" to help educate young people about intersectional climate justice, and they use teen ambassadors to spread the word at schools and recreation centers across the country. (FYI: They're always looking for new recruits!) Plus, members have given TV interviews, TED Talks, speeches, lectures, and even testimony in front of Congress to educate the public on climate change and demand government action.

In all of their appearances, the Zero Hour activists are both vocal and specific about their demands so that no adult can say, "I don't know what these kids want." You can find the complete list of science-backed demands on their website—the same list they took to their elected officials on July 19, 2018.

Carrying that list to Capitol Hill was the true beginning of their crusade. The next day, they celebrated the climate-justice community through an arts festival in nearby Dupont Circle. And the day after that—July 21, 2018—Zero Hour took to the National Mall for The Youth Climate March, joined by sister marches across the globe.

At this point, Zero Hour definitely has the attention of adults in power. The organization continues to organize strikes around the country, making sure to feature cities that will be hardest hit by climate change. But their biggest goal is to make themselves heard in upcoming elections. As many of Zero Hour's activists turn 18, they plan to ensure that climate change is a top issue and that any candidate not talking about it will answer to thousands of newly registered voters.

With everything that Zero Hour has accomplished, Jamie just laughs at the adults who still underestimate her. And she believes wholeheartedly that more young people need to find their voices, embrace activism, and get involved in creating the future they want for themselves. She's even written a book (*Youth to Power*, out in June of 2020) to help them do it. Why? Jamie herself says it best: "If only a handful of youth that started the #ThisIsZeroHour movement can have the impact that we had, imagine what millions of us can do! So young people, what are you waiting for? We've got work to do!"

FOLLOW THEIR FIGHT:
@ThisIsZeroHour on Facebook, Instagram, and Twitter

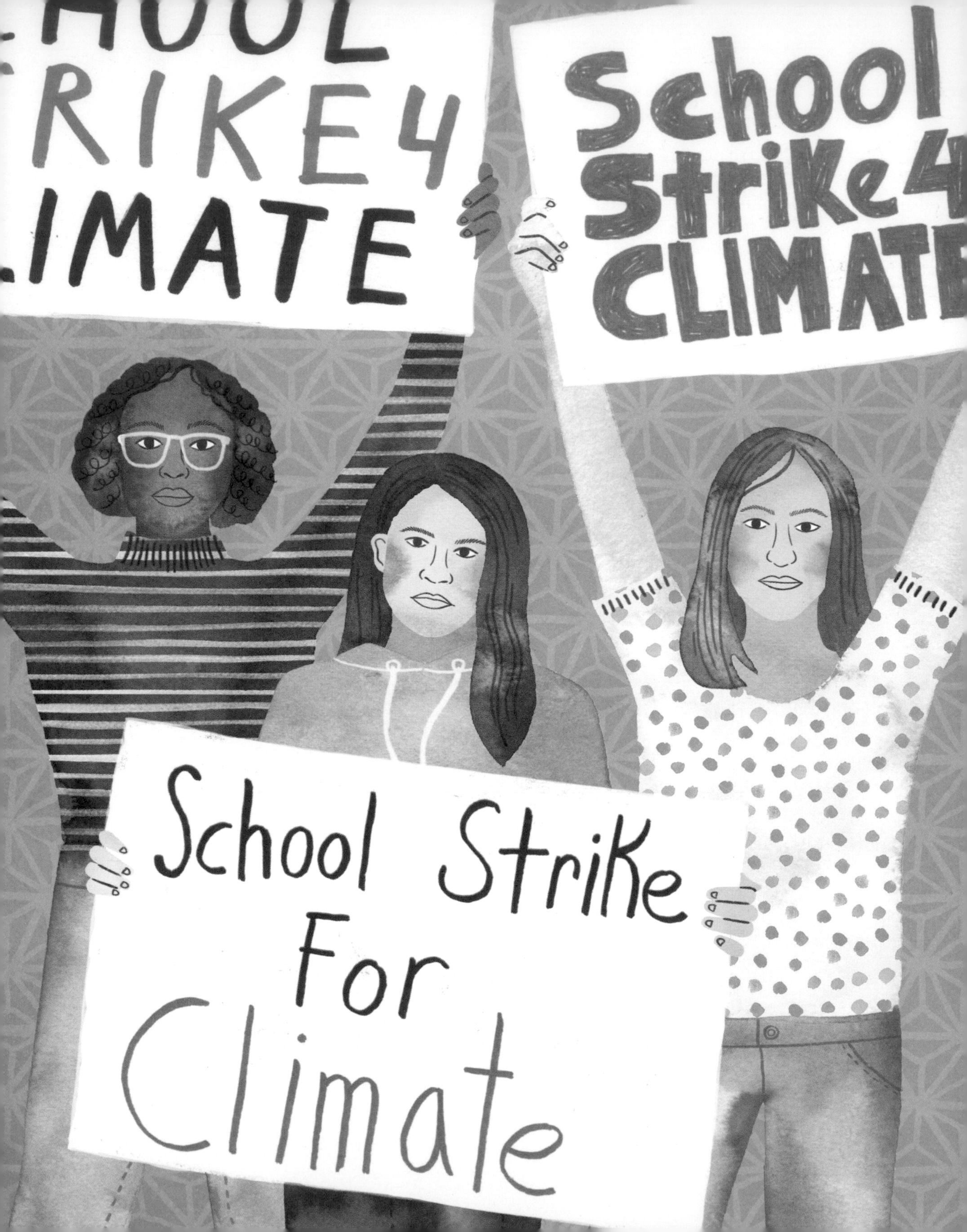
School
Strike4
CLIMATE
School Strike
For
Climate

THE US YOUTH CLIMATE STRIKERS

▶ Fighting for the Green New Deal, a comprehensive piece of legislation to fight climate change and inequality

▶ Petitioned for and approached presidential candidates about a climate debate, resulting in a televised town hall on CNN

IF WE DON'T STOP THE CLIMATE CRISIS SOON, THOSE ALREADY IMPACTED WILL BE HIT EVEN MORE AND GENERATIONS LIKE MINE WON'T HAVE A LIVABLE FUTURE. –ISRA HIRSI

For too long, being too young to vote made young people virtually invisible to the U.S. government. Now, young activists are elbow deep in politics and demanding change from the inside.

Take US Youth Climate Strike, for example. This is an organization founded by a 12-year-old (Haven Coleman) to bring Greta's Global Climate Strike stateside. She joined forces with 16-year-old Isra Hirsi and 13-year-old Alexandria Villaseñor not

THE ACTIVISTS

Even before starting US Youth Climate Strike, Haven (@havenruthie) attended town halls and held politicians accountable, Isra (@israhirsi) was working with Minnesota Can't Wait, and Alexandria (@AlexandriaV2005) was an active member of Zero Hour. USYCS brought them together and made them stronger. The current leaders of USYCS include Isra, Felíquan Charlemagne (@cfeliquan), Salomée Levy (@misa.misa1120), Maddy Fernands, Sabirah Mahmud (@sxbirah), and Karla Stephan. Haven and Alexandria have since stepped away from the organization, but both have big plans for addressing climate change.

only to organize marches but also to hold politicians accountable. As Alexandria said at the NYC march on March 15, 2019, "Change is coming, whether they like it or not. We will continue to push world leaders until they take climate action."

With their eyes on the 2020 presidential election, the USYCS activists focused on making climate change a part of the discussion. They amassed thousands of signatures on a petition for a climate debate and even contacted candidates directly. In the end, most of the candidates agreed, but the Democratic National Committee (DNC, the organization that hosts the debates) refused. More than that, the DNC threatened the candidates with expulsion if they entered into a climate debate. But the candidates heard the call of

these young activists, and they held a climate change town hall (essentially, an informal debate) on CNN.

The organization's desire to get the candidates talking about climate change goes beyond raising awareness for green policies. It's also about making sure that candidates will stand up to the kind of corporate greed that has ravaged the country, both environmentally and socially. A November 25, 2019, tweet from the USYCS account reads, "The Climate Crisis was not caused by the choices of individuals. This is a lie designed to make you feel guilty and powerless. It was

MILLIONS OF PEOPLE WILL BE DISPLACED, MILLIONS WILL STARVE, BILLIONS OF PLANTS, ANIMALS, AND ORGANISMS WILL GO EXTINCT. SO MUCH PAIN AND SUFFERING FOR ALL THE THINGS LIVING ON THIS EARTH—ALL MADE BY US. THIS IS A FIGHT THAT WILL DETERMINE LIFE AND DEATH FOR SO MANY; THIS IS A FIGHT THAT IS WORTH FIGHTING FOR. –HAVEN COLEMAN

> ## THIS IS NOT SOME ABSTRACT FUTURE ISSUE; THIS IS SOMETHING THAT'S HAPPENING IN PEOPLES' LIVES EVERY SINGLE DAY.
> —FELIQUAN CHARLEMAGNE

created by corporate greed, an economic system built on unchecked exploitation of the environment."

What the USYCS is referring to is the system by which the fossil fuel industry buys government support by donating to congressional campaigns. Congress doesn't have any incentive to move toward clean energy because the fossil fuel industry gives them job security. By holding politicians accountable, young activists are making it very clear that they don't play by the old rules. As they become old enough to vote, the only path to job security for Congress will be addressing their issues.

USYCS is "building a movement to take on the fossil fuel industry" while fighting for the Green New Deal, a program takes its name from President Franklin D. Roosevelt's New Deal, which was a series of public-works programs and financial reforms that helped the country recover from the Great Depression. The Green New Deal would help the country recover from both climate change and inequality.

Introduced by Representative Alexandria Ocasio-Cortez of New York and Senator

PLANET OR PROFIT

Killing the planet for profit isn't exclusive to America. Scroll through Youth Climate Strike's Instagram feed and you'll find a post exclaiming, "THE AMAZON IS BURNING." The post says, "This was not an accident. This was a result of corporate greed led by Brazilian President Bolsonaro, who advocates for the burning of land and making the Amazon profitable." The same thing is happening in Indonesia right now, where farmers are setting fires to clear land for palm oil production. Americans are contributing to the problem by buying items that contain palm oil. Reducing demand can make a difference. Eating less beef, consuming fewer paper products, and avoiding anything made with palm oil (check your soap) can help make clearing the land less profitable.

Edward J. Markey of Massachusetts, the Green New Deal program would wean the country off fossil fuels; curb greenhouse-gas emissions; ensure that clean air, clean water, and healthy food are basic human rights; and create high-paying jobs in clean energy industries for the working class. That last part—lifting up those who have been oppressed by the current system—is key. Without it, "oil barons turn into energy barons and workers are hurt all the same," says Ocasio-Cortez. Until they can vote for the Green New Deal, the members of USYCS will make sure that their representatives do.

FOLLOW THEIR FIGHT: @usclimatestrike on Twitter and Instagram

CHAPTER 4

LIFTING

EACH OTHER UP

SIMONE BILES

▶ The most decorated American gymnast of all time, with four signature moves named after her

▶ Founded a scholarship to help students around the world access higher education

WE CAN PUSH OURSELVES FURTHER. WE ALWAYS HAVE MORE TO GIVE. –SIMONE BILES

When you see Simone Biles run full speed toward the vault and whip through the air in twist after twist, you can't imagine anyone more fearless. She finishes with that thousand-watt smile, lighting up the arena and making you feel like her death-defying routine was a walk in the park. But, of course, that routine was the product of thousands of hours of training and pain—and yes, even fear.

Simone knows, maybe better than anyone, that being fearless doesn't mean not feeling fear— it means working through it. Practicing can help. So can having the support of friends, family, and professionals. But you have to be the one to do the heavy lifting. And you have to be the one to decide when you're ready to move forward.

When 146 young women confronted Larry Nassar, the USA Gymnastics doctor who used his position to sexually assault them, Simone wasn't ready. She couldn't move through the fear. She didn't want to admit to herself, let alone to her parents and friends, that this man had also assaulted her. She needed time.

TRY SOMETHING NEW

Simone discovered her love for gymnastics by accident, on a daycare field trip to Bannon's Gymnastix. A coach there noticed her imitating the gymnasts and immediately recognized her natural gift. He asked her parents to let her train with him, and the rest is history. Today, she's a four-time Olympic gold medalist and considered the most talented gymnast in the world. Imagine what gifts you could uncover if you just tried something new!

> ## BEING A GYMNAST MEANS HAVING THE STRENGTH TO HOLD ON AND THE COURAGE TO LET GO.
> —SIMONE BILES

So she watched as fellow gymnasts spoke in open court about how this man, their trusted team doctor, manipulated and abused them. And she listened to them question why their complaints to USA Gymnastics went unanswered, just like Simone's did. Finally, she cheered as Judge Rosemarie Aquilina sentenced Larry Nassar to up to 175 years in prison.

And then she was ready. In a letter posted to Twitter, she wrote, "I am not afraid to tell my story anymore," before stating that she, too, is a survivor of sexual abuse at the hands of Larry Nassar. In taking the time to process what was happening, Simone found the strength to say, "I know that this horrific experience does not define me. I am much more than this. I am unique, smart, talented, motivated, and passionate. I have promised myself that my story will be much greater than this and I promise all of you that I will never give up."

She also said that, for too long, she questioned whether the abuse was somehow her fault. "I now know the answer to those questions," she wrote. "No. No, it was not my fault. No, I will not and should not carry the guilt that belongs to Larry Nassar, USAG, and others." Simone realized that Nassar, like other sexual predators, had groomed her (the process of building a trusting relationship with the victim in order to manipulate, exploit, and abuse them in secret). In interviews, Simone has said that she wants all survivors to know: "It is not your fault."

Even while training for the 2020 Olympics in Tokyo and beyond, Simone works through her pain and confusion. "It feels like he took a part of me that I can't get back, so I'm still working on that part," she says, while admitting that she often just wants to cry or sleep. Although it's hard, Simone has proven to herself

PAYING IT FORWARD

You'll often see Simone's loving parents smiling down at her from the stands, sporting team colors in support of their astonishing daughter. What you might not know is that, although she calls them "mom and dad," they're actually her grandparents. When Simone was just 3 years old, she and her siblings found themselves in foster care after their mother, who struggled with drug addiction, lost custody. Simone bounced from home to home for three years, feeling unwanted as her mother tried and failed to overcome her addiction—until her grandparents adopted her and her sister.

It was thanks to them that Simone had the opportunity to discover her love of gymnastics and the coaches who would help her succeed. Knowing how lucky she was to be lifted out of a system where the odds are against you, Simone has made it her mission to pay that luck forward. In addition to partnering with the Mattress Firm Foster Kids program to provide clothing and school supplies to foster kids, she's joined with University of the People to provide them with a college education.

Simone chose to study at University of the People—a nonprofit, tuition-free, online university—for its flexibility. (It's not easy to train for the Olympics while cramming for exams!) But she chose to become its spokesperson because that flexibility gives students around the world easier access to higher education. "It's an opportunity for anyone who feels that the financial, structural, or personal barriers to college are too high for them to overcome," she says. And she knows that foster kids experience those barriers more than others—as few as 3 percent of them go on to earn a bachelor's degree. That's why she's also starting a scholarship fund to help pay for the University's application and assessments fees. "Our circumstances shouldn't define us or keep us from our goals, especially if that goal is higher education," she explains. "My hope is that I can help other foster-care children realize that goal in the months and years ahead."

just how powerful she is. "I'm strong," she says. "I'll get through it." One thing she is ready to do: win a gold medal on the balance beam.

Whether you're working through physical challenges or emotional ones, only you know what you're ready for and when.

When you can, push through the fear. When you need time, take it. And if you or someone you know has been sexually assaulted, ask for help. You can call the National Sexual Assault Hotline at 800-656-HOPE (4673) or visit RAINN.org/get-help to chat online or get the support you need.

FOLLOW HER FIGHT:
@Simone_Biles on Twitter and @simonebiles on Instagram

WE ARE the MAIN CHARACTERS of OUR LIVES.

MARLEY DIAS

▶ Started a campaign called #1000BlackGirlBooks to get stories with strong, black, female leads into the hands of students all over the world

▶ Wrote a book at the age of 13 encouraging kids to pursue their passion and use it to make the world a better place

EACH OF US HAS A MAGIC INSIDE OF US THAT WE CAN USE TO MAKE THE WORLD A BETTER PLACE. –MARLEY DIAS

You can read Wilson Rawls' *Where the Red Fern Grows* only so many times, right? That's what Marley Dias thought when she was assigned the book twice in two years. It wasn't just the repeat reading that bugged her, or even the book itself. It was that all of the assigned books felt the same. She came home that day and complained to her mother about having to read yet another book about "a white boy and his dog." But instead of just nodding or consoling her, Marley's mom asked her a question: "What are you going to do about it?"

That got Marley thinking. She realized that what she really wanted was to see stories with strong, black, female lead characters—girls like her—on the school curriculum. "I want to stop the intentional exclusion of some people's stories," she says, "and I want every child to have a place in literature where they can see themselves and learn about the experiences of others." So, in November

READING IS A LIFE SKILL

As a self-declared "book nerd," Marley can't imagine a life without reading. And she knows that books open you up to new ideas and possibilities, helping you to better understand the world around you. But she also knows that too many kids give up on reading because of *what* they're reading. For Marley, literacy, representation, and activism are all entwined, and that's why she created #1000BlackGirlBooks. She says, "My parents have taught me the value of reading and self-love through books that have characters that look like me and talk like me. I want to make sure other black girls around the world can see and love themselves, too, through these books." By helping kids find books that speak to them, she's opening them up to the lifelong love of reading she knows will help them learn, grown, and contribute.

of 2015, at the age of 11, she launched a campaign to collect and donate 1,000 books with black protagonists.

#1000BlackGirlBooks got off to a slow start, but Marley didn't give up. And today, she's collected more than 12,000 books. Did she just sit back and congratulate herself on a job well done? Of course not. She immediately started working toward a new goal of donating 1 million books to libraries, schools, and communities around the world. Because Marley gets it done.

In fact, that's the title of the book she wrote and published at the age of 13—*Marley Gets It Done: And So Can You!* For Marley, it was never just about the books. She says, "I want this book drive to teach other kids that they can do whatever they want to do. Anyone can change the world however they want for the better! This book drive is supposed to inspire bigger change." So, rather than encouraging kids to follow in her book-collecting footsteps, Marley's own book gives them clear and actionable steps to pursue whatever it is they're passionate about.

In her book, Marley urges her readers to get curious, to do more of what they love, and then to look for ways to create positive change. She wants them to be

MARLEY'S RECOMMENDED READS

Thanks to an ever-expanding reading list, Marley's favorites are constantly changing. But here are ten of her recommendations to get you started:

Another Brooklyn by Jacqueline Woodson

Aya: Life in Yop City by Marguerite Abouet

Brown Girl Dreaming by Jacqueline Woodson

Children of Bone and Blood by Tomi Adeyemi

From the Notebooks of a Middle School Princess by Meg Cabot

I'm Judging You by Luvvie Ajayi

One Crazy Summer by Rita Williams-Garcia

Please, Baby, Please by Spike Lee and Tonya Lewis Lee

The Hate U Give by Angie Thomas

The Sun Is Also a Star by Nicola Yoon

"upstanders" instead of bystanders—allies and activists who are working to make their schools and communities better and teaching their peers to do the same. "My advice to girls is to break those barriers," she says. "If you're the first person to speak out, understand that there are so many other girls out there that want to and by setting one example, saying one opinion, you can change the entire space."

Marley is certainly leading by example. In addition to starting the campaign and writing her book, she has given nationally televised interviews, organized a reading party at the White House, become the youngest editor at Elle.com, spoken at summits, and found herself on Forbes' "30 under 30" list. And she still has to find the time to finish her homework! But she wouldn't trade any of it because she knows she's making a real difference—for the kids who receive her donations and the kids who follow her into activism.

When you're feeling frustrated by something, what's your go-to move? Do you vent to friends? Complain to your parents? Talk to your teachers? It can be easy to shrug your shoulders and think, "It is what it is." But remember what Marley says: "Frustration is fuel that can lead to the development of an innovative

MOTHER KNOWS BEST

Marley's mom knew exactly which question to ask to get her daughter's creative juices flowing, and there's a good reason for that. Marley's mom is Dr. Janice Johnson Dias, president and cofounder of the GrassROOTS Community Foundation. She's made a career out of her activism, and she's always supported Marley's efforts to learn, grow, communicate, and create change. When Marley gets nervous or discouraged, her mother's always there with the same comforting advice: "What is there to lose? All you have to do is try your best. All you're going to do is gain. You're either going to gain knowledge from your mistakes or you're going to gain a new experience that you can tell your kids or that I can tell you when you're nervous again." Marley knows how lucky she is to have such a wonderful support system at home, and she's working hard to pay that encouragement forward.

and useful idea." So, the next time you're feeling fed up, try asking yourself, "What are you going to *do* about it?"

NO MATTER WHAT YOUR DIFFERENCES ARE, EMBRACE THEM AND BE PROUD OF THE WAY YOU ARE.

JAZZ JENNINGS

▶ One of the youngest people to be formally recognized as transgender and to act as grand marshal of the NYC Pride Parade

▶ Advocates for trans kids in life, on TV, in books, and now in movies

▶ Honored by LGBTQ+ organizations GLAAD and the Human Rights Campaign

NOW MORE THAN EVER, WE NEED TO CONTINUE TO USE OUR VOICES TO CREATE POSITIVE CHANGE, TO SHOW THAT WE EXIST, WE'RE HERE, AND THAT WE DESERVE TO EXIST FREELY. –JAZZ JENNINGS

Do you remember the first time you felt *different*? Maybe it was when you wore your new glasses to school or when someone called you a name. Or maybe it was when you got picked for the solo in music class and everyone heard your beautiful singing voice or when you placed first in the science fair. There's nothing wrong with being different. In fact, *being* different can help you *make* a difference.

Jazz Jennings knew she was different from day one, even before she had the words to tell anyone. But she found other ways to make herself clear, like pointing to her big sister and, eventually, stealing her pretty clothes. "I've always known exactly who I am," she says now. "I was a girl trapped

A PUBLIC TRANSITION

Being a teenager is hard enough, but imagine having to fight for the right to be the real you *on top* of dealing with hormones, homework, and human drama. Jazz bravely faced the physical realities of transitioning, *plus* the mental and emotional toll of those changes, all while dealing with life as a teen. And she's taken each exhilarating and exasperating step of that journey in the public eye. Why? Because she knows it's important for people to see a happy young woman who happens to be transgender. She doesn't care if it's TMI. "Yeah, it is personal and uncomfortable for some individuals," she says. "But how are we going to learn if someone doesn't step up to the plate and share their story?" By telling hers, Jazz is helping people embrace differences in themselves and in others.

A TRUE REFLECTION

If you only see people like you, it's hard to learn about anyone else. That's why it's so important that TV and movies reflect real life, with characters of every ethnicity, background, gender identity, and ability. By voicing a character in Hulu's pro-LGBTQ+ series *The Bravest Knight* and starring in Amazon Prime's *Denim* (a movie about a bullied transgender teen), Jazz is making sure that hers isn't the only LGBTQ+ story people hear and is helping to normalize what's actually already normal.

women and gender-nonconforming individuals are killed each year for being true to themselves. And even with the already painfully high rate of suicide among young people, LGBTQ+ youth are three times as likely to take their own lives because they feel they *can't* be themselves.

in a boy's body." Luckily for Jazz, her family saw and accepted her for who she really was. They supported her through her transition to living as a girl at the age of 5, using medication to block puberty at 11, and undergoing gender confirmation surgery at 17. Thanks to their love and understanding, Jazz finally feels like her true self.

And Jazz wants every other LGBTQ+ person to have the freedom to be true to themselves, too. The LGBTQ+ community faces an incredible amount of hatred, harassment, and discrimination. Too often, that discrimination leads to unemployment, poverty, homelessness, violence, and even death. Dozens of transgender

Jazz knows that she can't magically make the world safer for her LGBTQ+ family, but she's doing everything within her power to try. First and foremost, she's telling her story. In addition to shooting her TV show (*I Am Jazz*), Jazz has co-written a children's book by the same name and written a memoir called *Being Jazz: My Life as a (Transgender) Teen*. She's also given in-depth interviews to top journalists like Barbara Walters. By letting people peek behind the curtain of her life, she's helping them understand that *different* doesn't mean *bad*. And, as she says, "Change happens through understanding."

ONE OF MY BIGGEST HOPES IS THAT OUR NEXT GENERATION OF KIDS WILL GROW UP IN A WORLD WITH MORE COMPASSION." –JAZZ JENNINGS

Knowing that she's making a difference has helped Jazz blossom into a strong, vocal advocate for LGBTQ+ rights. First, she fought for her own rights to use the girls' bathroom and to play on the girls' soccer team. Writing a letter to the White House even earned her a meeting with then president Barack Obama. Now, with those victories under her belt, she's using her voice to fight for others. Jazz works closely with LGBTQ+ organizations like the Human Rights Campaign and GLAAD to bring awareness to issues of equality, safety, and acceptance.

For the LGBTQ+ community, Jazz is not only an ally but also an example of the light at the end of the tunnel: a happy, healthy, and safe LGBTQ+ person. Even though she herself faced discrimination, bullying, threats, and medical complications, she wouldn't change any part of her journey. "If I could go back in time and be born as a girl, I would not do it, because I'm proud of who I am and

THE IMPORTANCE OF SELF-CARE

Even while transitioning and changing the world, Jazz never let her grades slip. She earned the title of valedictorian of her high school and admission to Harvard University. But when all of that hard work led to burnout, she realized that she needed to make room for some downtime, too. Now, she listens when her inner voice tells her to slow down. She manages the stress of her brave and busy life by listening to music, meditating, taking a walk outside, and petting her animals. Another helpful tip of hers involves setting tech boundaries. "Unless you're using the phone for something positive and for a connection with other people or to make yourself feel good, then just don't use it at all," she says. So, when social media is making you more anxious than happy, take Jazz's advice and put the phone down!

what I've accomplished," she explains. "And I hope that by sharing my story, I can help everyone else understand that they should be proud of who they are as well."

FOLLOW HER FIGHT: @JazzJennings_ on Instagram and Twitter and @Jazztrans on Facebook

KAVYA KOPPARAPU

▶ Founder and CEO of the Girls Computing League, a nonprofit dedicated to fostering girls' interests in science and technology

▶ Traveled to Vienna, Austria, to deliver a TEDx Talk on the future of medicine

I STRONGLY BELIEVE THAT AGE IS JUST A NUMBER. HAVING A YOUNG PERSPECTIVE HAS REALLY ENABLED ME TO VIEW THE FIELD AS HOW IT CAN BE IN THE FUTURE, NOT HOW IT IS RIGHT NOW. –KAVYA KOPPARAPU

Have you found that *thing* that you love to do more than anything? The thing that you're so happy doing that you lose track of time? (No, scrolling through Instagram doesn't count. But taking beautiful photographs to post to Instagram does.) If you haven't found it yet, don't worry. You will. And one way to help you do so is to follow your curiosity. What are you curious about? What makes you wonder? What keeps popping into your head?

Kavya Kopparapu has turned following her curiosity into a super-productive habit. Not only did she found her own nonprofit, she also made huge contributions to computer programming and medicine—all before she turned 18! Every impact she's made has started with a question. But that makes sense with Kavya, because she's always been a scientist at heart.

In fact, it was her love of biology and medicine in middle school that led Kavya to her first question: How do you analyze data? To learn the answer, she attended a workshop at the National Center for Women & Information Technology, where she discovered computer science. From that moment on, she was hooked.

Kavya taught herself how to code over one summer, completely entranced by the process. "My mom would say, 'You know you have to eat,'" she remembers, "and I was like, 'No, this is so interesting!'"

When the schoolyear came, she skipped into freshman AP Computer Science at her high school, which happens to be a science magnet school that specializes in technology.

SILVER LININGS

You might think that Kavya spent her whole childhood in front of a computer, but she was actually an avid lacrosse player. She spent three or four hours each day practicing. But when she tore her ACL and couldn't play anymore, she didn't wallow. She immediately put those hours to good use, creating her Girls Computing League. In fact, that's why she called it a league. She wanted her organization to have the same sense of community she felt when playing team sports. The next time you suffer a disappointment, ask yourself how you can make it work for you. Your tough break could inspire a whole new chapter!

That brought her to her next question: Why were there only five girls in a class of thirty people? "If this is a situation in an advanced school, what would this be like in an area where people didn't have the resources?" she wondered. Kavya learned about the gender gap in technology (the fact that the tech industry is dominated by men), and then she set out to close it.

Kavya founded the Girls Computing League, a nonprofit dedicated to "empowering, educating, and encouraging girls and their [computer science] interests through workshops, coding clubs, and large-scale events." The organization's goal is to increase diversity in tech by bringing tech education to students who might not otherwise have access, including young girls, racial minorities, and students in low-income areas. "I want to make an impact on students who want to pursue computer science and make them more confident in their abilities, skills, and future," says Kavya. After all, computer science opened up a whole world of answers for her.

When Kavya read an article about Senator John McCain, who was battling glioblastoma (a kind of brain cancer), questions started to form again. "I read that glioblastoma rates of survival had not improved in the past 30 years," she says. "I was like, 'We're in such a technological era, where we know so much more about cancer than we did back then, so why aren't we getting better at treating these patients?' I just ended up in this wormhole of reading research papers, articles, talking to oncologists and pathologists." And then it hit her: She could use computer science to speed up the process of creating targeted cancer treatments.

With her remarkable coding skills, Kavya created a program that can instantly analyze scan slides of cancerous brain tissue and call out what's unique to that patient. Done the standard way, that would take scientists weeks of tests and analysis—weeks that are precious to a cancer patient—and the results might still not be as accurate and in-depth as what Kavya's system can discover in seconds. GlioVision, as she called the platform, is now in clinical testing at Georgetown University. Kayva, herself, is studying computer science at a different school—Harvard. Considering all that Kavya's done in high school (and that includes inventing a 3D-printed lens system and a mobile app that can diagnose diabetic retinopathy, a complication of diabetes that can lead to blindness), the world can't wait to see what she does in college!

JUST ASK

All of the young activists in this book have done incredible things using their own passions, talents, and skills. But none of them has been alone in a cause. Creating large-scale change means knowing when to ask for help. Kavya came to understand that firsthand. When she wanted to start the Girls Computing League, she had no money or resources. So she reached out to women in the field whom she admired. To her surprise, every one of them responded and helped make GCL a reality.

So, when she realized the impact her GlioVision platform could have for cancer patients, her next move was to contact scientists in the field. Kavya couldn't have gotten GlioVision off the ground without them. That's why she tells others, "Don't be afraid to ask people for the things you need or for help. The worst thing they can say is no, but on the flip side, all it takes in one person to change the game. Always ask."

FOLLOW HER FIGHT:
@KavyaKopparapu and @girlscomputing on Twitter

NADYA OKAMOTO

▶ Founded PERIOD, an organization dedicated to fighting menstrual inequality, at 16

▶ Launched a yearlong campaign and a National Period Day to help fight period poverty at the national level

▶ Wrote *Period Power: A Manifesto for the Menstrual Movement* to encourage future activists

> **YOUNG PEOPLE HAVE THE POWER TO ADD SIGNIFICANT CONTRIBUTIONS IN BOTH CREATING AND IMPLEMENTING SOLUTIONS, AND WE WILL BE THE ONES TO CARRY ON THE LEGACY OF CHANGING IDEAS. —NADYA OKAMOTO**

You've probably seen those bright and bubbly ads for period products on TV. Maybe you've shopped for products yourself and noticed the endless variety of cups, tampons, pads, and cleansers. So, how often do you talk about periods? If you said, "Never," you're not alone. But Nadya Okamoto is going to change that. She's been working hard to start a national conversation about menstruation since she was 16 years old.

Two years earlier, Nadya discovered that not talking about periods was hurting people—specifically homeless women.

A QUICK REFRESHER

Just looking at the cost of period products, the lack of access to them, and the stigma around them, you might think that periods are optional. They're not. They're actually an important part of a life-giving biological process—the one that makes pregnancy possible. The process includes the uterus growing its lining to make things comfy for a fertilized egg, then shedding that lining (which is actually tissue, not blood) when there is no fertilized egg. And considering the lovely side effects—cramps, bloating, headaches, and bad moods—most menstruators wish periods were optional. But again, they're not. And without them, none of us would be here.

MAYBE NOT APPENDICITIS

When Nadya got her first period, she thought she was dying. She had had stomach pains all week and was convinced she had appendicitis. So, when she used the bathroom and saw blood, she assumed the worst. Nadya ran downstairs to say a dramatic goodbye to her mom (as only a tween can), but she didn't get the reaction she expected. Her mom laughed and yelled, "You're a woman!" That was the day that Nadya learned that periods are just a natural, annoying part of life.

Her own family had just lost their home, and her commute to school went from a quick 10 minutes to 2 hours on a city bus. She took that extra time to get to know the homeless community she now felt a small part of, and what she learned was that access to menstrual hygiene products was one of the largest hardships the community faced.

Nadya listened to the stories of women using "toilet paper, socks, grocery bags, cardboard, and paper to absorb their menstrual blood," knowing the discomfort and infections that would cause. The more she researched the issue, the more flabbergasted she felt. Nadya learned that, incredibly, period products aren't considered necessities. They're taxed in more than 30 states, they're excluded from school bathrooms, and they're not covered by government-assistance programs like food stamps.

Although she was homeless, Nadya was fortunate—she never wanted for necessities. Knowing that others weren't as lucky made her determined to help. At first, she used the money she earned from babysitting to buy extra period products for the women along her route. Then, she organized a donation drive in her community to support the local homeless shelter. And when she discovered that no organization in the United States was addressing menstrual inequality, she founded one.

No big deal, right? Well, it's actually a huge deal. PERIOD has become more than an organization—it's a movement. Its youth activists work to normalize the conversation around periods and to distribute period products to those in need, using its network of nearly 600 chapters on campuses all over the world to deliver its message and goods. And thanks to those chapters, PERIOD is now the largest youth-run nongovernmental women's health organization in the world.

Distributing period products to those in need is incredibly important work, but it's just the beginning. Nadya has big plans for her growing foundation. In July of 2019, she announced PERIOD's yearlong campaign to fight period poverty at the national level. "The way we need to make long-term systemic change is to change the system itself," Nadya says.

Her first priority was raising awareness and getting people talking about periods, which she definitely did during the first annual National Period Day on October 19, 2019. That day saw thousands of people turn out for 61 rallies held in all 50 states and four countries to demand an end to menstrual inequity and period shaming.

Now that the word is out, the next step is to help create legislation requiring that "clean and healthy period products must be freely accessible in schools, shelters, and prisons." Then, she wants to tackle the "tampon tax" (state sales tax on menstrual products) in all 50 states. And to top it all off, Nadya is holding nationwide donation drives to collect menstrual products for those in need.

Nadya has gone from barely being able to say the word "period" to giving speeches and TEDx Talks about period poverty all over the country. All it took was believing that she could make a difference and that that difference was worth making. The next time you come across a problem worth solving, just think of one small thing you can do to help. You never know where that idea might lead you!

MORE THAN AN INCONVENIENCE

For those of us with the money for and access to menstrual hygiene products, periods are little more than an inconvenience. For those with medical conditions like endometriosis, "that time of month" can be unbearable. But for those who can't afford period products, periods can lead to poverty, unemployment, homelessness, and even death. That may sound extreme, but using unsanitary products or not changing period products often enough can lead to serious, life-threatening infections. And missing school, work, job interviews, and more because you're worried about bleeding through your clothes can keep you from succeeding in life. These consequences are all too common, and they don't need to be. As Nadya says, "Menstruation isn't something that [should] hold anyone back from discovering and reaching their full potential." She's doing everything in her power to make sure it's not.

FOLLOW HER FIGHT: @nadyaokamoto and @periodmovement on Twitter and Instagram

JADEN SMITH

- ▶ Started his own sustainable bottled water company at the age of 17 to help stop single-use plastics from littering the ocean

- ▶ Helped create a portable water filtration system to bring clean water to communities without access

MY GOAL IS TO MOTIVATE AS MANY [OF MY GENERATION] AS I CAN TO BECOME SOLUTION-BASED ACTIVISTS. –JADEN SMITH

When catching waves one day off the California coast, 11-year-old Jaden saw firsthand that plastic water bottles were a problem—they were bobbing in the saltwater right alongside him. Some kids might join a beach cleanup or start a recycling program. But Jaden had a different idea. Instead of just working around the problem, he decided to solve it. Luckily for him, activism runs in the family. He turned to his famous (and famously kind) father for help, and together they quietly created JUST Water.

Jaden set out to make bottled water better and more sustainable at every level, starting with the water itself. He partnered with a family friend to bring the company to Glens Falls, New York, a small town with plenty of water to spare

from natural mineral springs. While some companies are happy to bleed natural

ALL IN THE FAMILY

Jaden grew up in a family of multitalented people. His parents, Will Smith and Jada Pinkett Smith, are both wildly successful actors, entrepreneurs, and philanthropists who have encouraged their kids to make an impact. Through the Will and Jada Smith Family Foundation (WJSFF), they've created a space for each family member to champion a cause and make a real difference. Jaden's dad believes that, "If you're not making someone else's life better, then you're wasting your time. Your life will become better by making other lives better." Follow the family's fights: @officialWJSFF on Instagram.

springs dry, Jaden uses only 3 percent of the town's *excess* water—water that's easily replenished by rain and snow. Plus, he's providing the town with new jobs and the funds to fix old, leaky pipes that lead to water waste.

For JUST's container, Jaden chose to skip the bottle altogether. Instead, he created cartons that are made from 82 percent renewable resources (materials that grow back) and are 100 percent recyclable and refillable. The paper in each carton comes from certified-sustainable forests. The caps are made from sugarcane, which regrows every year *and* absorbs carbon dioxide. And because the packing is printed flat and folded later, JUST only needs one truck to ship 1.5 million cartons (versus 13 trucks for 1.5 million plastic bottles), reducing harmful emissions by 74 percent! In other words, every single aspect of JUST's carton fights climate change.

Creating an eco-friendly company from scratch turned out to be perfect prep for Jaden's next challenge: the Flint Water Crisis. For years, the residents of Flint, Michigan, have lived without running water. Well, the water was running fine, but it was brown, foul smelling and tasting, and making people sick. That's because the city cut costs by changing their water source from Detroit's clean system to

THE PLASTIC PROBLEM

Plastic water bottles are made from a toxic substance called petroleum—yep, the same stuff that fuels cars. And petroleum is responsible for nearly half of all greenhouse gas emissions (a huge contributor to the climate crisis), plus oil spills that harm wildlife. This is a huge problem, because:

- People use 500 billion water bottles *each year*.
- 80 percent of plastic water bottles end up in landfills.
- It takes 450 years for a single bottle to decompose.
- Plastic makes up 90 percent of the garbage floating around in the ocean.
- That plastic has collected to form five massive islands of garbage.
- Floating plastic kills more than 1 million marine animals each year.

And now that it's found its way into our food and water, the average American eats up to 142 microparticles of plastic every day. Choosing sustainable alternatives like JUST Water and refillable stainless-steel water bottles is one of the only ways to bring those numbers down.

the Flint River, an unofficial dump site for waste and raw sewage. But because Flint is a mostly poor, mostly African American city, government officials ignored complaints for an unbelievable 18 months.

With the help of doctors, scientists, journalists, and activists, the Flint community exposed the government's racism and neglect. Companies like JUST stepped in to provide bottled water, but Jaden knew Flint needed a long-term solution while they fought for officials to do the right thing. He put all of his water knowledge to work to create one: a portable water filtration system called the Water Box.

Jaden's device, which he created with engineers and activists, has four levels of filtration and produces up to 10 gallons of clean drinking water per minute. He partnered with First Trinity Missionary Baptist Church, which distributed more than 5 million plastic water bottles during the first months of the crisis, to bring the Box to Flint. Now, instead of relying on donations of small bottles, residents can just refill their big, blue, eco-friendly jugs.

Jaden never let his age stop him from making a difference. He considers it an asset. "My generation and the next generation are the solvers. My goal is to

SPREADING LOVE (AND FOOD)

On his 21st birthday, Jaden launched his newest nonprofit initiative: I Love You Restaurant. The popup food truck delivers JUST Water and delicious vegan meals to people in need. I Love You Restaurant got its start in Los Angeles, a community in which up to 60,000 people are homeless and one in five people don't know where their next meal is coming from. But Jaden won't stop there. He plans to take the truck nationwide to help the 40 million people who don't have access to affordable, nutritious food. Follow the truck's stops: @ILoveYouRestaurant on Instagram.

motivate as many as I can to become solution-based activists," he says. He travels to schools to spread that message, telling students, "I just want you to know that I came up with [JUST Water] when I was your age, and that means you have the infinite ability to come up with any idea or any way that you want to change the world." Believing you can is the first step.

FOLLOW HIS FIGHT:
@jaden on Twitter and @officialjaden on Facebook

CHAPTER 5

TAKING CARE OF EACH OTHER

HAILEY HARDCASTLE

▶ Helped create and pass a bill in Oregon requiring mental health days for students

▶ Hopes to encourage kids to treat their mental health like they do their physical health

THE WHOLE EXPERIENCE OF PASSING THE BILL, IT MAKES YOU REALIZE YOU CAN CHANGE THINGS. YOU DON'T HAVE TO HAVE SPECIAL CONNECTIONS. YOU JUST HAVE TO SPEAK UP AND BE PASSIONATE. –HAILEY HARDCASTLE

Between climate change, school shootings, politics, and bullying (not to mention soaring college costs and the pressure of extracurriculars), students today clearly have a lot more on their minds than schoolwork. If you ever find yourself feeling overwhelmed, anxious, or depressed by any of it, know that you're not alone.

Mental health advocate Hailey Hardcastle has been there herself, and she knows the importance of having a good support system in place. When all of that pressure led to a panic attack during school, her mom didn't think twice before pulling her out with a fake excuse about a doctor's appointment. And after a day of rest, Hailey felt great.

A STICKY STIGMA

A stigma is a negative or shameful belief that's usually wrong, unfair, and born out of fear or misunderstanding. Mental illness has a long history of being stigmatized. Centuries ago, it was seen as a sign of evil or witchcraft. Today, it's sometimes considered a weakness. But mental health *is* physical health. Anxiety, depression, panic attacks—these are all products of chemicals in the brain. You can't control having a mental health condition any more than you can control having asthma or allergies. All are medical conditions, and all need to be treated that way. Little by little, advocates like Hailey are chipping away at the stigma and helping people get comfortable talking about mental health. If you suffer from a mental health condition, you have absolutely nothing to feel ashamed about.

You might be asking yourself, "Why did Hailey's mom have to lie?" Hailey asked herself the same question, and it's what led to her changing how the school systems in Oregon treat mental health. In June of 2019, Oregon Governor Kate Brown signed into a law a bill requiring mental health days for students. Hailey not only advocated for that bill, she helped write it. And it's one of the first state laws *ever* to treat mental health and physical health equally.

Hailey knew that she wanted to do something, but it wasn't until she heard Parkland survivor David Hogg speak about student activism at the Oregon Association of Student Councils summer camp that she and other campers realized they *could* do something.

During workshops on student life and mental health, they started talking about the need for designated mental health days. Hailey joined with fellow students Sam Adamson, Lori Riddle, and Derek Evans, plus pro bono lobbyists, to draft the language for House Bill 2191. "We were inspired by Parkland in the sense that it showed us that young people can totally change the political conversation," Hailey says. "Just like those movements, this bill is something completely coming from the youth."

In addition to helping write the bill, Hailey and others had to advocate for it at the state capitol. In her testimony there, Hailey said, "House Bill 2191 is important to me because it would reaffirm the idea that mental illness is no different than physical illness, and it would offer support to the masses of students that are struggling with mental health challenges every day."

Although Hailey received a lot of support for her bill, there were plenty of naysayers. Some said the policy would give kids an excuse to skip school. Others said the legislation wasn't necessary because kids could already take time off for mental health—they just had to lie or pretend to be sick. But Hailey helped them understand how dangerous those lies could be. "Why should we encourage lying to our parents and teachers?" she said. "Being open to adults about our mental health promotes positive dialogue that could help kids get the help they need." Teaching kids to be ashamed of their mental health issues could have deadly consequences.

At least two Oregon parents agree, saying that Hailey's law might have saved their daughter. Jason and Roxanne

REACH OUT

Suicide is the second-leading cause of death for young people between the ages of 10 and 24. If you or someone you know is struggling, remember that *you are not alone*. There are people in your life who care about you and want to help. Don't be afraid to talk to them.

No matter what is going on in your life—whether you're facing family conflict, mental health issues, pressure at school, bullying, loss, or a struggle with sexual identity—you can get through it with support. Don't keep your struggle to yourself. Opening up to others not only can lift some of the burden off you but also can help you discover treatments and coping techniques.

If you feel like you can't talk to family or friends, talk to a trusted teacher or counselor at school. Or call the National Suicide Prevention Lifeline at 1-800-273-TALK (8255). They offer free, confidential support—day or night. You can also find helpful resources and chat with someone on their website, www.suicidepreventionlifeline.org. Worried about someone else? They can help with that, too. Whatever you do, don't keep your pain bottled up. Talking to someone could make all the difference.

Wilson's 14-year-old daughter Chloe took her own life in 2018 after being bullied for coming out as bisexual. When things were rough at school, she would pretend to be sick to stay home. "Because she lied to get her absences excused," explained Roxanne, "we didn't get to have those mental health conversations that could have saved her life." Chloe was one of five teens near her hometown of Eugene, Oregon, to commit suicide that month alone.

In fact, suicide is the second-leading cause of death for young people. And in Oregon specifically, the suicide rate is 33 percent higher than the national average. For Hailey, that's all the more reason for legislation that takes mental health seriously. She hopes that her bill will "help identify the students who are already missing school for mental health reasons" so that parents and teachers will be aware of the issue and can offer help.

House Bill 2191 wasn't the only legislation that Hailey hoped to see pass. She had also pushed for schools to offer mental health checks alongside the eye exams that start in elementary school. The bill didn't pass the first time around, but Hailey's not giving up. She knows that mental health checks can save lives. In the meantime, she and her fellow activists are helping other states lay the groundwork for mental health days. They hope to see the initiative go nationwide.

FOLLOW HER FIGHT: #mentalhealth and #suicideprevention on Twitter

SAMEER JHA

▶ Wrote a book called *Read This, Save Lives: A Teacher's Guide to Creating Safer Classrooms for LGBTQ+ Students*

▶ Founded The Empathy Alliance, an organization dedicated to creating safer schools and communities for LGBTQ+ youth, at age 14

DON'T BE A BYSTANDER. WHATEVER PROBLEM YOU SEE, WHATEVER ISSUE YOU ARE PASSIONATE ABOUT, TAKE A STAND AND DO SOMETHING ABOUT IT. –SAMEER JHA

Wherever you are in school, you can probably name a favorite teacher or counselor. Did they make math easy or brighten your days? Were they your sounding board when you were going through a tough time? When you spend most of your time at school, a good teacher can make all the difference. Without that support, LGBTQ+ advocate Sameer Jha might never have had the courage to be themself. And now they're paying that kindness forward by educating educators in LGBTQ+ issues and helping them become allies for their students.

Sameer started school as a little boy who loved pink and Disney princesses, in an educational environment that was overwhelmingly homophobic. By middle school, Sameer was used to being bullied. "I always felt like I was doing something wrong. Like I needed to hide who I really was. Like I should be ashamed, which I was," they say. But a counselor's simple suggestion to look into an independent high school changed everything.

At their new school, Sameer discovered their first Gay-Straight Alliance (GSA) club, met openly LGBTQ+ faculty members, and learned about gender fluidity from new friends. This newly supportive community gave them the courage to come out as queer and nonbinary—identifying as neither male nor female and adopting the pronouns they, them, and their—at age 14. Realizing what a difference that supportive environment made, Sameer founded The Empathy Alliance (www.theempathyalliance.org) to make other schools safer and more inclusive for LGBTQ+ students. And what better place to begin than Sameer's middle school?

With the help of faculty and staff, Sameer started the school's first GSA, helped provide LGBTQ+ friendly books for the library, and held school meetings about bullying prevention. Their message of love and empathy quickly spread to the entire school district, where they helped secure an inclusive health-education curriculum for fourth grade and up. That initiative ensured that 35,000 students in 43 schools received education on LGBTQ+ identities. Today, The Empathy Alliance has reached over 1 million people.

Sameer believes that "awareness and education are the two most effective tools for fighting bias." That's why they educate the public any way they can—through keynote speeches, workshops, interviews, radio shows, panels, op-eds, and events on topics ranging from bias management, bullying, trans rights, and the gender binary to starting a GSA, coming out, and understanding intersectionality. They also collaborate with national LGBTQ+ organizations on special projects to promote queer youth well-being. "Whether I am working on a social

A CLOSE-KNIT COMMUNITY

As the child of South Asian immigrants, Sameer was raised in a close-knit community that shared their family's culture and traditions. "My parents thought that this would make it easier for me to grow up in America, living in a bubble of saris and samosas within a mostly white country." But that culture came with a destructive undercurrent of homophobia, and Sameer became its target. "I was a really gay child. Like, really gay," they joke today. As much as Sameer's parents tried to help them conform, they naturally stood out.

Sameer thanks their teachers for encouraging them to discover a different community—a progressive school where Sameer could be themself. That community helped them feel confident enough to come out to their South Asian community.

Sameer was lucky to have incredibly supportive parents who advocated for them to the rest of their small community, but they know that not everyone is that fortunate. They want other Asian LGBTQ+ youth to know that, "your ethnicity and culture don't have to conflict with your queerness. If your family isn't affirming of your identity, know that you don't have to give up your culture to be yourself. There are queer-inclusive places of worship, cultural organizations, and even families who will welcome and love you."

AS A QUEER PERSON OF COLOR WHO TRACES MY HERITAGE TO A COUNTRY IN WHICH HOMOSEXUALITY IS PUNISHABLE BY DEATH, I WANT TO USE MY PRIVILEGE AS AN AMERICAN CITIZEN WITH A SUPPORTIVE FAMILY TO RAISE AWARENESS AND FIGHT FOR THE PEOPLE WHO CAN'T. –SAMEER JHA

media campaign, speaking on a panel, or facilitating a small workshop," Sameer says, "my goal is to change hearts and minds through education and awareness."

Although The Empathy Alliance has been an incredible tool for creating LGBTQ+ allies in the school system, Sameer isn't finished paying forward the support they received. They also want to advocate for safer schools from the inside, as someone's favorite teacher. Sameer is attending Stanford University with plans to do just that.

WHY PRONOUNS MATTER

How annoying would it be if someone continued to call you Robert when you've already said you prefer Bobby? Or if they got it completely wrong and called you Ronald for an entire conversation? Now imagine if you corrected them, and they decided they were more comfortable calling you Robert. That's downright rude.

Just as using a person's name is a sign of respect, so is using that person's preferred pronouns. As we learn more about the fluidity of gender, we've come to understand that not everyone fits neatly into conventional gender roles. Sameer, for example, is nonbinary (meaning they don't identify as male or female) and prefers *they*, *them*, and *their* pronouns. If you're not sure which pronoun someone prefers, don't be afraid to ask respectfully, just as you would ask for someone's name.

FOLLOW THEIR FIGHT: @sameerjha2001 on Twitter and Facebook

SAM ORLEY

MAX ROTHMAN

WOLVERINE SUPPORT

SAM ORLEY AND MAX ROTHMAN

▶ Former leaders of the University of Michigan's Wolverine Support Network, an organization dedicated to the mental health and well-being of students

▶ Founded The Support Network to expand the WSN peer-to-peer support model to high schools and colleges across the country

▶ 2018 JED Student Voice of Mental Health Award Honorees

VULNERABILITY AND EMPATHY ARE CONTAGIOUS, AND THEY START WITH US. –MAX ROTHMAN

One of the most impactful things you can do is open up to others about how you're feeling. Not only does it ease your own burden, it also reduces stigma and gives others a chance to see their own burdnens as well. That's because everyone experiences feelings of anxiety, sadness, depression, and inadequacy at some point or another. It's part of being human. And sharing an experience is how we process it and move forward.

But opening up about those feelings is also one of the hardest things to do, thanks to the stigma of mental health issues. And that's something that Sam Orley and Max Rothman have worked

hard to change. They both know first-hand the benefits of asking for and receiving support.

As University of Michigan students, Sam and Max were both dealing with the pain of losing someone. Max had lost a friend to a tragic accident in middle school, and Sam lost his older brother to suicide just months before he started

college. Although their losses were different, they both knew that they wanted to foster an environment of support on their college campus.

In the Wolverine Support Network, they found exactly what they were looking for: an organization that provided, as Sam says, a "refreshingly vulnerable, empathetic, and inclusive space accessible to all University of Michigan students to be themselves and talk openly and honestly." WSN offered

weekly meetings led by trained student facilitators as well as campus-wide events to help students blow off steam and build supportive relationships.

Sam and Max believed that having the support of peers, as opposed to staff or counselors, was particularly helpful. Although the group leaders had gone through rigorous training, they were also just college students. They could relate to everything that their peers were going through. As student Evelyn Wallace put it, "I've found a place on campus where people not only know my whole story but are looking out for me and empowering me to pursue what I really care about, while at the same time helping me feel appreciated even on the days when I have difficulty getting myself to class."

IT'S OK TO NOT BE OK

Many people have lost someone to suicide. And the reaction from those who knew and loved them is often that they had no idea their friend was suffering.

Sam has said that's one of the hardest parts about his brother's death—knowing that he had suffered in silence. That's why Sam has worked tirelessly to help other students open up and let them know that it's OK to not be OK. If you're unhappy, anxious, depressed, or having thoughts of suicide, *you are not alone*. There are other people feeling the same way, and there are people who want to be there for you and help you through it.

If you don't want to talk to friends or family, check with your school or community for support services. And if you're contemplating suicide, call the National Suicide Prevention Lifeline at 1-800-273-TALK (8255) to get immediate support.

BODY IMAGE AND BOYS

We tend to think of body image as something that only girls struggle with. But photoshopped models and impossibly fit Instagram influencers can make anyone feel bad about their body. When Max came to the University of Michigan, body image was one of the issues that concerned him. And thanks to his training as a peer leader, he knew enough to share how he was feeling with his fraternity brothers.

Fraternities have their own set of problems—the pressure to conform often contributes to body issues and anxiety. But the conversations that Max started led to the creation of a mental health chairperson and an outlet for all of the fraternity members to discuss their own struggles. After seeing the positive impact this had on his fraternity, Max helped establish the position in all other fraternities belonging to the Interfraternity Council Chapters. Just by opening up himself, Max made a difference in countless students' lives.

Sam and Max recognized the importance of that feeling of peer support. For Max, it was the support he, himself, received after his friend's accident. For Sam, it was the support he wished his brother had had. And both realized that students across the country could benefit from it. So, they set out to recreate WSN at high schools and college campuses across the nation.

Together, they created The Support Network, which offers schools "the blueprint and advisory to launch an effective peer-to-peer support model with student leaders, working jointly with administrators." They hope not only to provide all students with the support they need but also to start a national conversation about mental health and well-being. To that end, they've spoken at conferences and events to raise awareness for the program.

Sam and Max know that feeling comfortable talking about mental health needs to become the new normal. Not only would it alleviate the anxiety and stress that everyone experiences, it could also put an end to the feelings of helplessness and hopelessness that lead to suicide. Everyone, student or adult, needs to know that they aren't alone, that there's nothing wrong with them, and that help is there if they need it.

FOLLOW THEIR FIGHT: @umichwsn and www.thesupportnetwork.org

SATVIK SETHI

▶ Working to make the world a happier place, one person at a time

▶ Developing the Runaway platform, which provides positivity and support to those who are struggling

I'VE SEEN A LOT OF PEOPLE BATTLING WITH MENTAL HEALTH PROBLEMS, AND I JUST WANT TO MAKE SURE I'M DOING MY BEST TO BRING POSITIVITY INTO PEOPLE'S LIFE AND ENCOURAGE THEM TO PAY IT FORWARD. –SATVIK SETHI

Have you ever been working on an assignment late at night and accidentally gone down an Internet rabbit hole? You know, when you start looking up the dogs of World War II for your history paper and end up watching video after video of huskies talking back to their owners? Before you know it, hours have gone by and you haven't done anything productive. (We've all been there.) But one late night in 2014, Satvik Sethi's rabbit hole took him in another direction— one he never expected. He went from looking up quotes on Instagram for an assignment to saving lives.

INVISIBLE BATTLES

We know now that just because you can't see physical symptoms of an illness, that doesn't mean the illness doesn't exist. People suffer silently with a number of health conditions—multiple sclerosis, migraines, fibromyalgia, diabetes, and Crohn's disease, to name just a few. The same goes for mental health: The fact that you don't see the problem doesn't mean there isn't one. You have no way of knowing what someone is dealing with unless they choose to tell you. So just be kind, always. Offer a warm smile and a compliment. Sit quietly and listen. Ask how you can help. A simple act of kindness could make all the difference for someone who's struggling.

"IF YOU SEE SOMEONE STRUGGLING, IT DOESN'T MATTER IF THEY'RE YOUR FRIENDS OR FAMILY, JUST PUT OUT A HELPING HAND."

—SATVIK SETHI

Satvik lost one of his closest friends to suicide in ninth grade, the day he "first realized the devastating impact that mental health could have on someone." So that night, when he was scrolling through Instagram and found an image of someone self-harming, he couldn't move on. He had to help. "I immediately reached out to this stranger online and told them that if they needed someone to talk to, that I was there to listen—and just like that, they reached out to me and told me about their struggles. That night, I spoke to about six people and continued to talk to them until they felt better."

After spending four hours being a sounding board for strangers that night, Satvik decided to make a habit of helping. He went looking for people who were struggling and offered to talk. One day, he realized that he had helped 150 people. And instead of feeling accomplished, he decided that he needed to do more.

Satvik began developing Runaway, a social entrepreneurial venture that he hopes will help people improve their mental health. It consists of a website full of positivity resources, events to increase mental health awareness and advocacy, and an app that will pair users with a chat bot or trained volunteers. (The app is still in development.)

The venture is called Runaway because so many of the people Satvik spoke to said they wanted to run away, and he hopes that his program will be a safe place to run away to. Many of the strangers Satvik helped have become

MENTAL FITNESS

You go to gym class (whether you want to or not) to stay healthy and fit. You know that you're supposed to fuel your body with whole, nutritious food. And you do what you can to feel comfortable in your own skin, whether that's working out or wearing your favorite hoodie.

But with all of that focus on physical health, you can forget sometimes how important it is to take care of your mental health. That means actively choosing positivity over negativity and giving yourself a break when you need to. Do things that make you happy, eat delicious food, read positive affirmations, plan for an event you're looking forward to, or just relax and watch a funny movie. Do what you can to feel comfortable in your own *mind*.

Satvik is programming that kind of positivity directly into his app so that you'll always have it at your fingertips when you need it. (While you wait for Satvik to finalize the app, you can visit Runaway's Instagram page or website, www.runawayapp.com/positivity-zone, for a happiness boost.) But also remember that apps like Runaway can only do so much—they're not a replacement for therapy. If you need more help than an affirmation can give you, reach out to a support group or therapist in your area. It may take a while to find the right fit, but your mental health is worth the effort.

friends, and he's been able to see the impact his kindness has had on them. "It's great to see some of them become immensely successful at work—as writers, photographers, artists, and corporate executives, among other great jobs," he says. "Some of them recently got into or graduated from prestigious colleges, and it's an amazing feeling to see them do well, and to know you were there for them when they were so close to giving up."

Through the platform and his own late-night chats, Satvik hopes that people remember this: Nothing is permanent. Even when it feels like the end of the world, you're just getting started. "As long as you stay strong, and as long as you keep going, things will change, and they will change for the better. I promise you."

FOLLOW HIS FIGHT:
@runaway.app on Instagram and @runaway_app on Twitter

HAILE THOMAS

▶ Advocates for the health benefits of a plant-based lifestyle through social media, YouTube videos, conferences, television appearances, and TEDx Talks

▶ Founded a nonprofit at the age of 12 to engage, educate, motivate, and empower young people to make healthy lifestyle choices

WHEN YOUNG PEOPLE ARE FUELED WITH FOOD THAT IS NOURISHING AND ENERGIZING, THEY'RE ABLE TO BECOME THEIR BEST SELVES. –HAILE THOMAS

When your family is running from work and school to soccer practice and choir rehearsal and a dozen other things, pizza or fast-food cheeseburgers sound like a great idea. Who has time to make a salad with all that going on? And be honest—you'd rather have the pizza anyway.

It's not always easy to reach for the healthy options first, but bad eating habits are having a big impact on Americans and their health. Armed with some nutritional know-how, fixing that problem is within reach. Luckily, Haile Thomas has made it her mission to help.

GOING VEGAN

Although Haile became a healthy eater when she was 8, she didn't become vegan until a few years later, when she was about 13 years old. She started by challenging herself to try it for a few months, but the change stuck and spread. "Then my family joined me," she says, "and together we learned about the movement as a whole, the ethical and environmental benefits, and how you can take a stand for something just by what's on your fork." Haile knows that there are a lot of misconceptions about veganism, including "the perception that vegans only eat grass, juice cleanses, and smoothie bowls." That's why she's shared dozens of delicious vegan recipes on her website and YouTube channel. She hopes they'll entice others to adopt a healthy, animal-friendly, and environmentally conscious plant-based lifestyle.

THE FIRST LADY IS A FAN

Can you imagine being able to say that the First Lady of the United States is one of your biggest fans? Haile can. Mrs. Obama has said that "Haile is an example for all of you, what your little, powerful voices can do to change the world." Not only did Haile create one of the winning entries for Michelle Obama's first White House Kids' State Dinner (a quinoa salad with corn and black beans), she also had the honors of introducing the First Lady for the second annual dinner and joining her at the 2013 State of the Union.

Haile is in awe of the former First Lady, saying, "She's such a genuine, comforting, and loving person, and the attention and care that she puts into acknowledging young people in general is so uplifting. Within five seconds of being near her, you feel like you're part of the family, or important, or special, and doing something that matters." The mutual admiration makes sense—Haile's mission goes hand in hand with the First Lady's Let's Move! initiative, which aimed to reduce childhood obesity and encourage kids to live a healthy lifestyle.

Haile learned the power of proper nutrition when her father was diagnosed with type 2 diabetes. She was 8 years old and already a whiz in the kitchen, thanks to her mother's lessons. But after the diagnosis, the whole family realized they needed to overhaul their diet and lifestyle. Those healthy changes helped Haile's father reverse his disease.

> ## IF YOU DON'T DOUBT YOURSELF, THEN YOU DON'T REALLY LEAVE ROOM FOR OTHERS TO DOUBT YOU.
>
> **-HAILE HARDCASTLE**

This experience taught Haile that food is not only fuel but also medicine. By eating well and making healthy lifestyle choices, you can combat a number of health conditions, including obesity, heart disease, and—yes—diabetes. Haile was hooked.

The more she learned about food and nutrition, the more she yearned to share that information with others. So, at just 12 years old, Haile founded HAPPY (Healthy Active Positive Purposeful Youth) to educate at-risk kids about nutrition through cooking classes, summer camps, and in-school programs. "This peer-to-peer connection was super important to me," she says. "I wanted to bring what I had learned into my community as a sort of low-cost nutrition education that's fun and engaging and nutritious."

You might think founding a nonprofit is enough, but Haile has even more achievements under her belt. In 2015, she became a nutrition science assistant at the Canyon Ranch Institute. In 2016, she partnered with the nonprofit organization Harlem Grown to provide education in urban farming, sustainability, and nutrition. In 2017, she graduated as the youngest Integrative Nutrition Health Coach from the Institute for Integrative Nutrition. And by spring of 2020, she'll have published her own cookbook: *Living Lively: 80 Plant-Based Recipes to Activate Your Power & Feed Your Potential*. Haile won't stop until she's changed how the whole country feels about food!

HEALTHY EATING IS A HUMAN RIGHT

Have you ever noticed that a fast-food hamburger costs a lot less than a fresh salad? That makes it hard to stay healthy when money is tight, and it's one of the reasons that low-income areas tend to suffer disproportionately from medical issues like obesity and diabetes. Low-income communities also tend to be food deserts, or areas that don't have access to affordable and nutritious food because there isn't a supermarket nearby. People who live in food deserts often have to rely on convenience stores and fast-food restaurants to meet their nutritional needs.

That means that, right now, healthy eating is treated as a privilege when it should be a right. And the first step in creating the change needed is talking about it. When Haile discovered that low-income and minority communities were more likely to suffer from diet- and lifestyle-related illnesses, she knew that she could make a difference. That's why her organization is dedicated to bringing nutritional education to underserved and at-risk youth. Although her priority is giving kids the tools they need to live their best lives, she also hopes to start a larger conversation about the importance of access to good nutrition.

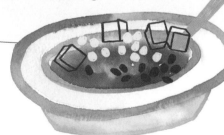

FOLLOW HER FIGHT: @hailevthomas on Twitter, @hailethomas on Instagram, and @hailethomas1 on YouTube; and @thehappyorg on Twitter and Instagram

ABOUT THE
AUTHOR AND ILLUSTRATOR

KATE ALEXANDER is a writer, editor, and book lover. She is inspired by the fire and activism of Generation Z and by anyone else who stands up for what they believe in. She lives in Manchester-by-the-Sea, Massachusetts.

JADE ORLANDO has loved art for as long as she can remember. After a childhood spent doodling cats and mythical creatures, she studied Illustration at SCAD and set off on her journey as an illustrator. Her colorful work has been featured in books, apparel, advertising, and children's products. Jade lives in Atlanta, Georgia, with her husband, greyhound, and four cats. When she's not illustrating, you can usually find her curled up with her pets and a really good book.